When the storms of life shake us to our very core and doubts creep in, what is your foundation? *FaithLift* gives a fresh, biblical perspective, challenging us to rely on faith rooted in the Lord rather than in our feelings. As you read of the testimonies of those in the Bible, as well as stories of today, your faith will not only be strengthened, but the knowledge of truth you will glean from this book will, in turn, encourage you to share your faith with others.

—KAY ARTHUR, CEO AND COFOUNDER
PRECEPT MINISTRIES INTERNATIONAL

Babbie's pen sings with insights. Her notes of truth lift my faith and help harmonize my daily walk. Come join the concert!

—PATSY CLAIRMONT
WOMEN OF FAITH SPEAKER AND
AUTHOR, *THE SHOE BOX*

Reading *FaithLift* is like sitting in Babbie Mason's kitchen, girlfriend to girlfriend, sipping on some Georgia peach tea and talking about the stuff that really matters. Her open, honest writing style makes you feel right at home. Her biblical principles and real-life examples gently convict, even as they nudge you forward in your own faith walk. Babbie's heart for God is on every page, and she asks nothing of her readers she hasn't put into practice herself. Trust me, sis; you'll be blessed if you get a *FaithLift*!

—LIZ CURTIS HIGGS
BEST-SELLING AUTHOR, *BAD GIRLS OF THE BIBLE*

Weaving her own personal experiences through the fiber of God's Word, Babbie creates a brightly colored vision of hope for all of us. *Anyone can become a champion of faith!* It is often through the simplest and least expected followers of His that the God who IS, DOES move heaven to earth in response to faith. This is a *FaithLift* that stays firm forever!

—Sandy L. Smith, Director and Founder
Balancing the Demands of Life
Retreat Ministry for Women
Bailey Smith Ministries

Faith is believing that it is so, even when it is not, so that it may be so. My friend Babbie not only writes about it here, but she epitomizes it in her personal life, family life and professional life.

—Anthony T. Evans, Th.D.
Senior Pastor, Oak Cliff Bible Fellowship

Babbie, in her warm, personable style, lifts our hearts, educates our minds and stirs our spirits into a practical faith that prevails! She proves that you can walk with kings yet not lose the common touch. Babbie has made faith touchable!

—Dr. Dale C. Bronner, Senior Pastor,
Author, Businessman
Word of Faith Family Worship Center,
Atlanta, Georgia

I have just read *FaithLift*, and it is truly Babbie! She loves to share stories to encourage and inspire, and I know readers will be blessed by *FaithLift*.

—Greg West, Producer
Babbie's House

As long as I have known Babbie, she has expressed confidence in God through her writing and through her singing. In this book, she uses insights gleaned from her personal experience to encourage and motivate us to trust our God in any season and in any situation. Whatever the circumstance, Babbie's faith will energize you to trust in God.

—Dr. Lois Evans, Senior Vice President
The Urban Alternative

In her book *FaithLift*, Babbie eloquently states biblical truths that encourage us to live by faith and not by sight. She suggests key ingredients that we can apply in everyday life to help us stay focused on God's truth.

I've known Babbie for almost thirty years now, having been her college classmate. The only thing that I can see that has changed in her since those early days of ministry is that she has memorized more of the Bible! She is genuine and lives what she writes about.

—Julie Baker, President/Executive Director
TimeOut for Women!

One of the things that is most apparent about Babbie whether she is speaking or singing is the woman is a worshiper who leaves a lasting effect on all that encounter her ministry! This quality translates to this marvelous work.

FaithLift will challenge you to translate your worship into everyday living in practical and real ways that will positively affect the lives of others around you and take your own faith to higher heights.

—Michelle McKinney Hammond, Author
How to Be Blessed and Highly Favored

Perhaps you've questioned what real faith is all about because it seems so ambiguous. Question no more! Babbie shares her practical, personal, powerful experiences of faith with what the Bible says about faith. She links them together to give clear, concise, complete and creative answers to your questions. Once you've read this book, you will never question the conduct and commitment to a life that has a *FaithLift*.

—THELMA WELLS, PRESIDENT,
A WOMAN OF GOD MINISTERS
SPEAKER/AUTHOR, WOMEN OF FAITH CONFERENCES
PROFESSOR, MASTER'S DIVINITY SCHOOL
AND GRADUATE SCHOOL

Faith is one of the backbone fundamentals of Christianity. Without it, we are unable to experience all that this walk we are on has to offer. My friend Babbie has done an unparalleled job of making clear this often-misunderstood phenomenon of faith. She has made it clear to the reader why it is needed and, most importantly, how it can be practically used and experienced. I have been challenged and changed because of the material she has written, and you will be, too.

—PRISCILLA SHIRER, AUTHOR
A JEWEL IN HIS CROWN

Faith Lift

PUT WINGS TO YOUR FAITH WALK AND SOAR

BABBIE MASON

Charisma®
HOUSE

FAITHLIFT by Babbie Mason
Published by Charisma House
A part of Strang Communications Company
600 Rinehart Road
Lake Mary, Florida 32746
www.charismahouse.com

Scripture quotations marked THE MESSAGE are from *The Message*, copyright 1993, 1994, 1995, 1996. Used by permission of NavPress Publishing Group.

Scripture quotations marked TLB are from The Living Bible. Copyright © 1971. Used by permission of Tyndale House Publishers, Inc., Wheaton, IL 60189. All rights reserved.

Cover design by Rachel Campbell
Interior design by David Bilby

Library of Congress Cataloging-in-Publication Data

Mason, Babbie.
Faithlift / Babbie Mason.
      p. cm.
ISBN 0-88419-960-6 (trade paper)
1. Faith—Biblical teaching. 2. Christian life—Biblical teaching.
I. Title.
BS680.F27 M37 2003
234'.23—dc21
                    2002154271

    03 04 05 06 04 — 8 7 6 5 4 3 2 1
        Printed in the United States of America

To my loving husband, Charles.
Your commonsensical approach to
life puts faith on display. Your love
and support down through the years
go beyond what words can say.

T HE HEARTBEAT OF faith is to possess the vision long before holding the object of that vision in your hands. Dreams and visions rarely come to pass until you wake up and go to work. I am grateful to so many who saw this book before they actually held it in their hands. So many wonderful people were willing to sow seeds of faith and work tirelessly to reap this labor of love I call *FaithLift*.

Many thanks to Charisma House for your faithful support and this great privilege of laboring with you. Thanks to Barbara Dycus, not only for your editing work but also for your encouraging words. Thanks to Rachel Campbell for the beautiful cover design and to photographer Donna Permell of Atlanta, Georgia, for helping me to put my best face forward. A special thank you to all who shared their life's story on the pages of this book; I believe the accounts of your life will catch the sails of many discouraged hearts that have been dashed by life's storms. Many thanks to Phyllis and Lavonne, at Babbie Mason Ministries, for doing such a great job of organizing my life.

To my mother, Mrs. Georgie Wade, and in memory of my precious father, Reverend Willie G. Wade (1922–1987): Thank you for a great heritage of faith that I not only hold dear to my heart but also I gladly pass on. To my sister, Benita, and my brothers, Pastor Ben, Alan and Matt: I greatly admire your gifts and your deep faith in Christ. To our son Chaz: You are a treasure to your parents and a gift to the world. To our son Jerry, daughter-in-law Jessica, and granddaughter Layla: What a joy to see some of our visions for you come to fruition. Continue to pass the faith along.

To you, the reader: What an honor it is to share my heart with you. May these words whet your appetite for more of Christ, causing you to dig deeper into the Word of God. I pray the result will be a richer life, anchored by a deeper faith. Instead of being aimlessly carried away by life's tempests, be reminded to let the winds of adversity carry you to a new level of trusting in the Lord. Sail on, my friend. Sail on!

To my Lord and Savior Jesus Christ: This walk of faith is one day marching to victory, and on another day, I admit, it's stumbling in blind faith. Whether in joy or pain, I find my faith in You is what sustains me through it all. For this, I am grateful. In this, I can rest.

Contents

Faith
Forward

ALL AROUND ME I hear dismal news about the church. While I share some of the concerns, I see a wonderful work of God rising like the morning sun on the ocean horizon. This glorious work is still in such infant stages that I think perhaps it's most visible to those who travel and serve in many different dimensions and denominations in the body of Christ. A profoundly important revival is beginning to take place, but not quite like we expected. We want breadth. Numbers. More people saved! And so does God. But He has another work He wants to do within the church that will cause us to be far more effectively used for breadth. It's called *depth*. Specifically, a depth of sanctification and a depth of faith. The combination invites God to do the inconceivable like no other.

I am convinced God is calling the church in our generation to a revival of faith. Though there are pocket exceptions, the corporate body of Christ has suffered incalculably from unbelief. I'm not even sure we've had the faith to believe Scripture enough to face the horrific gap between our theology and our reality. Furthermore, many of us have allowed the misuse of the concept to become our excuse for not practicing faith. The good news is that faith—the authentic New

Testament kind—is beginning to come back in style.

I'm not talking about name-it-and-claim-it theology. I'm talking about simply believing God is who He says He is and can do what He says He can do. I'm talking about learning to abide in Christ and letting His words abide in us so that our petitions begin to reflect His heart and mind (John 15:7–8). The result is a God-glorifying harvest that bears witness to a lost world that Christ is alive and powerful. Ultimately, the harvest will be one of souls. I am convinced that *breadth* revival will follow closely on the heels of a *depth* revival.

FaithLift, written masterfully by my friend Babbie Mason, is powerful evidence of God's call to a revival of authentic, biblical faith. We don't have to wait for our entire congregations to experience revival. We can each have a revival of our own and let the Holy Spirit spread a fire of joyful faith in our midst. (Joyful because good news shared in a bad mood tends to lessen its effectiveness.)

FaithLift is a great place to begin your own revival of faith. Its author is the essence of Psalm 45:1: "My heart is stirred by a noble theme as I recite my verses for the king; my tongue is the pen of a skillful writer." Babbie writes out of a heart stirred by the Holy Spirit, and she undoubtedly possesses the pen of a skillful writer. My blessed sister has the God-given ability to make a point both beautifully and practically. A rarity indeed.

Maybe I'm just partial. After all, I love her dearly. But I'm convinced that if Christ tarries, Babbie Mason will go down in church history as one of the most anointed voices of our generation.

—BETH MOORE, AUTHOR AND SPEAKER
LIVING PROOF MINISTRIES

About
Faith

A S I LOOKED in the mirror the other day, I stuck my neck out and pulled up my sagging chin. With the fingers on each hand, I raised up the wrinkles on my forehead. I lifted the skin at my temples to smooth out the crinkles around my eyes. Then I declared to myself, "Face it, Girlfriend, you could use a face-lift. Before you start to go downhill, you need some upkeep!"

Well, a face-lift is out of the question. I've earned every one of these wrinkles, and I'm not about to get rid of the proof that proclaims to the world, "I'm an overcomer!" Recently a good friend of mine told me concerning her bulges, wrinkles and rolls, "If you can't hide it, decorate it." So I'll dab on a little more wrinkle cream, put a little more makeup on this face and decorate it with a smile.

You may or may not be to the place where you need a face-lift. But no matter how smooth or wrinkled you may be on the outside, our hearts can always use a *FaithLift*, a little reconstructive surgery for the soul. There's always room for an encouraging word to elevate our emotions, pull us out of our problems and help us to soar above our circumstances to a new level of believing. That is what faith will do. It turns things around and heads us in the right direction.

In each chapter of this book you will be reminded that if God can use ordinary people like Moses to hoist the hopes of an entire nation, He can use you in extraordinary ways. If God can use a simple shepherd boy like David to slay a defiant giant named Goliath, He can certainly supply you with the strength to raise the roof of courage in your life. God used a young, single, unmarried girl by the name of Mary to bring our precious Savior and Redeemer, Jesus the Christ, into the world. And God can surely equip you to step up to the difficulties you face, look them in the eye without fear, defy the odds and watch a miracle be born in the face of impossibility.

Look at God's track record along your own journey, and decide that you will continue to trust Him when all seems lost.

We have a lot in common, you and I. We cook. We clean. We love husbands and raise children. We celebrate our friendships. But we also face health challenges. We worry about our children. We get frustrated with marriage. I know you experience all these things because I've met you out there on the road. During a concert in Dallas, I saw you wipe away a tear. I hugged your neck and kissed your baby in Brooklyn. I heard your story after my concert in Boise. I received your letter in the mail. That's how I know you hurt as I do sometimes. And that's why I believe with all my heart that this book will offer a word of hope. I believe it will bolster your faith and blow a fresh breeze of faith-filled anticipation into your heart's sails.

I pray this book will encourage you. But I believe it will challenge you, too. Life is filled with circumstances that bog us down, down to the doldrums—so far down that we forget that we do not have to go there. We do not have to live beneath our privilege as believers when Christ has lifted us up to heavenly places. I believe this book will challenge you to walk away from doubts and fears, to run with a new confidence. Anew and afresh, you will be reminded that God's Word can work in your life. Read a little at a time, or read it all in one sitting. But as you read, look for God's thumbprint on your life. Remember your own stories. Look at God's track record along your own journey, and decide that you will continue to trust Him when all seems lost.

Each chapter is a labor of love, just as I labor over the lyrics and melodies of the songs that God has given me to write. I hope the words on each page will cause your heart to hum a tune of delight or to hone a word of encouragement to speak light into someone else's dark world.

My heart's desire is that you will see Christ in a new way and decide that when you can't feel Him with your feelings, you will feel Him with your faith. Read on, and allow these words to become a concert of faith that will raise your hopes to the rafters.

Now faith is the substance of things hoped for, the evidence of things not seen.

—HEBREWS 11:1, NKJV

CHAPTER 1

Faith

First

D O YOU REMEMBER when you were very small and Christmas morning was slowly approaching? If you were like me, the day couldn't come fast enough. You anticipated each day because it was one day closer to Christmas morning. When it finally arrived, you knew that under the tree were wonderful gifts wrapped just for you with your name on them. You had enough experiences in the past to know that each gift you opened was going to be just what you needed. There were even some wonderful gifts that contained some things that you wanted as well.

Faith is a lot like that. You can know by experience and with a certainty that God is who He says He is, and He will do everything He promised He would do. Faith comes into operation when you don't see those promises taking place, yet you believe that they will come to pass. Let's break it down like this.

> ☕ "Now faith is…"—Faith brings the promises of God into the present.

> ☕ "The substance of things hoped for…"—Faith always waits patiently for God to answer and holds out hope against all odds.

☕ "The evidence of things not seen…"—Faith always believes the best, although physical evidence may prove otherwise.

To get the big picture of *what faith is*, let's look at the Father of Faith himself, Abraham. God made some promises to Abraham and told him to look forward to some awesome things:

> Lift up your eyes from where you are and look north and south, east and west. All the land that you see I will give to you and your offspring forever. I will make your offspring like the dust of the earth, so that if anyone could count the dust, then your offspring could be counted. Go, walk through the length and the breadth of the land, for I am giving it to you.
>
> —GENESIS 13:14–17

Abraham had some important choices to make. He didn't know it then, but the future of an entire nation rested on this one decision. He could have stayed right where he was, in a comfort zone. But Abraham chose to be obedient. He left the land where he lived, parted company with his family members and struck out on a journey into the land of the unknown to venture out on faith.

Who would have ever believed that Abraham would become a father at such an old age? Look at his wife, Sarah, too. But just as God promised, Abraham was able to hold the fruit of his promise in his arms at one hundred years of age. Sarah, the object of a miracle as well, conceived and gave birth to Isaac when she was ninety years old. God promised Abraham that he would become a father. Not the father of one son, but the father of an entire nation of Jewish people, who occupy the nation of Israel to this day.

As I look at the faith of Abraham and apply its precepts to

my own walk of faith, I've unearthed some nuggets of truth concerning faith. This is *what faith does.*

> *A simple act of faith produced what the natural could not produce— a miracle.*

FAITH BELIEVES THE IMPOSSIBLE

In all actuality, ninety-year-old women and one-hundred-year-old men can't have children. But God's promises always defy natural law. In the natural, water does not part upon command. But that is exactly what happened in Exodus 14:13–14, another account where God's chosen one believed the impossible. The enemy was in hot pursuit of the entire nation of Israel, which was under the leadership of Moses. Pharaoh and his Egyptian army followed fiercely behind them in horse-drawn chariots, intending to kill them all. The people of God found the enemy breathing down their backs and the Red Sea looming out in front of them. Trapped, the Israelites began to blame their leader as they complained and cried out in fear.

But Moses wasn't filled with fear—*he was filled with faith.* This was Moses' faith-filled response:

> Moses answered the people, "Do not be afraid. Stand firm and you will see the deliverance the LORD will bring you today. The Egyptians you see today you will

never see again. The LORD will fight for you; you need only to be still."

—EXODUS 14:13–14

Read on in verses 21–22:

> Then Moses stretched out his hand over the sea, and all that night the LORD drove the sea back with a strong east wind and turned it into dry land. The waters were divided, and the Israelites went through the sea on dry ground, with a wall of water on their right and on their left.

Moses' obedience was the first step toward witnessing a move of God on the Israelites' behalf. A simple act of faith produced what the natural could not produce—a miracle. The people of Israel crossed over the Red Sea safely. Moses stretched his hand back toward the sea, and the great wall of water came crashing down upon Pharaoh's army. They were all drowned in the depths of the sea. Time and again I've heard it said, "God can make a way where there is no way." And he can. All he needs is activated faith.

In July of 2002, our nation came to a standstill as we watched the news story of nine miners who were trapped in the Quecreek Mine in Eastern Pennsylvania. Two nine-man crews had entered the mineshaft on a Wednesday night, just as they did each night. One crew was working near the end of a shaft, and the other at a different location. Suddenly one team accidentally broke through the earth into an old 1950s mineshaft that had long been abandoned. It was filled with water. Instantly, more than fifty million gallons of water came rushing in on the crew near the end of a shaft, while the second crew raced through neck-high waters to escape to safety.

Rescue workers and equipment swarmed the scene with unfailing determination in an effort to reach the miners trapped two hundred forty feet beneath the earth. Family members and fellow mine workers gathered at the site as the rescue operation continued. No one knew whether the men trapped below were dead or alive. For the next seventy-two hours, rescue workers labored around the clock while family members prayed and held on to their faith unceasingly.

One of the first steps the rescue workers took was to drill a hole into the mine precisely where the miners were located. Then they inserted a pipe to introduce fresh oxygen into the mineshaft. Immediately, rescue workers heard tapping sounds vibrating back against the pipe. This let them know that the miners were still alive! Rescue workers and family members stood by holding their breath, looking for the smallest signs of life. They were determined to believe for the best. The rescue workers began pumping warm air into the mine and to draw out the cold water.

Rescue workers knew that at least some of the men were alive. Their pace quickened. Drilling a rescue shaft to the men couldn't begin until more than twenty hours after the accident when a drill rig arrived from West Virginia. Drilling had to come to a halt on Friday morning when a fifteen-hundred-pound drill bit broke after hitting hard rock about a hundred feet down. The rescue effort was delayed for nearly eighteen hours.

In spite of setbacks, rescue efforts continued. Little by little rescuers grew closer to reaching the miners. The rescue shaft finally broke through into the mine chamber two hundred forty feet underground. Rescuers removed the drill and lowered a headset and a light into the mine in order to communicate with the miners.

Within minutes it was confirmed to the spellbound spectators that all nine men were alive! One by one, the men were lifted out of the dark, dank cavern to safety. The soot-covered face and bright-eyed smile of the first miner being lifted to life again is indelibly stamped on the memories of those who were there or who watched by television. The crowds shouted as each of the other miners was lifted up and out!

One woman at the scene was the daughter of one miner and the wife of another. She told news reporters that she prayed throughout the entire ordeal; she knew she could not lose a dad and a husband. She just knew in her heart that it wasn't their day to die.[1]

Faith always believes the impossible. That is what loved ones were believing as they looked on at the rescue operation over those three days. That is what believers all over America were doing as they watched the rescue efforts by television. They were praying for a favorable outcome in what looked like an impossible situation.

*Faith always believes
the impossible.*

When circumstances seem to have risen over your head and you are buried beneath the rubble of doubt, remember that God is bigger than your problems and that all things are under His feet. When you are in trouble, and your adversary, the devil, is seeking to devour you, cry out to God. He will hear you and deliver you. Psalm 34:6 says, "This poor man called, and the LORD heard him; he saved him out of all his troubles." Isn't it good to know that God is as close as the mention of His name? The strength you need is just a prayer away. Psalm 138:3 reminds us:

When I called, you answered me; you made me bold
and stouthearted.

FAITH SEES THE INVISIBLE

Yes, faith sees that which is not evident. Faith sees the sick
healed. Faith believes lost family members will be saved. Faith
sees tumultuous relationships turn toward peace. Faith envisions difficult battles won.

In Numbers 13, Moses sent out twelve spies to explore the
land of Canaan, the land God had promised to the Israelites.
Ten men came back with a negative report. They saw the
inhabitants of Canaan as giants in the land. And they saw
themselves as grasshoppers. (See Numbers 13:29–33.)

Only two men, Joshua and Caleb, came back with a report
that encouraged the people of Israel to act on what God had
ordered them to do—see the invisible, realize the possibilities
and move in to possess the land.

*Fix His promises in your
heart before the battle begins.*

At a women's conference recently, I heard the testimony of
Heather Mercer and Dana Curry, two young American women
who were in Afghanistan with a missions organization. They
were making an effort to help the war-torn nation combat
homelessness and help the poor. They were captured in
Afghanistan and imprisoned by the Taliban for sharing their
faith in Christ. If convicted of proselytizing, they could face the
death penalty. Getting a fair trial would be next to impossible.
Their statements were altered, and the list of charges against

them was falsified. While in prison, they lived in fear for their very lives. Threats were made to them, and they heard bombs falling all around them—bombs that were being dropped by their own American government.

In order to dispel their doubts and fears, they spent time praying to God for deliverance and encouraging each other in the Word of God. In the early days of their captivity, they were not allowed to have their Bibles. They spent those first few days encouraging themselves and one another by quoting God's Word from memory and by singing hymns and praise songs. At times they endured the pitfalls of discouragement. But on the other side of discouragement, and upon their release from prison, they surfaced with a deeper and greater faith.

Oh, what a compelling thought. In order to meet your daily challenges head-on you must be proactive. You must have the weapons of the Word of God, the power of prayer and the joy of praise active and effective in your life. They must already be in you. Imagine being imprisoned for your faith and not being granted the privilege of having your Bible in your hand. Would you have enough of it already stored away in your heart to recall it from memory, word for word? It is so important that you have a strong, unwavering belief that God will do what He says He will do. Fix His promises in your heart before the battle begins. Then you will be able to stand strong when you don't yet see the outcome.

FAITH PRACTICES THE IMPRACTICAL

God often tells people to do things that we would consider, in our natural senses, to be totally ridiculous.

> God's prophet Elisha told Naaman, a man with leprosy, that in order for him to be clean, he must

go and wash seven times in the dirty Jordan River. (See 2 Kings 5.)

Jesus tells us that in order to be rich, we should give everything away. Our natural tendency is to hoard all we can get. But Luke 6:38 tells us otherwise: "Give, and it will be given to you..."

The Lord spoke to the tribe of Judah, telling them that in order to win the battle over their enemies, they must march into the battle singing victory songs (2 Chron. 20:21).

Jesus commanded Lazarus, a man who had been dead and in his grave for four days, to come out of the grave to live again (John 11:43).

In real life, real men don't walk on water as Peter did in Matthew 14:29.

Faith practices the impractical. Faith will almost always contradict your feelings. Have you ever been in a valley of decision where your faith was telling you to do one thing and your feelings were telling you to do another? Your feelings are controlled by your emotions, which cannot always be trusted. Your faith is founded upon unchanging biblical principles, which can always be trusted. A very wise woman once told me, "When you can't feel God with your feelings, feel Him with your faith."

Even though I have no desire to fly an airplane, the flying process has always intrigued me since I find myself in the air on a regular basis. I had a hunch that flying an airplane was very much like walking by faith.

Think about it. On an average flight two hundred people board an aircraft with their luggage and personal belongings. Most of these passengers know nothing about the concept of aerodynamics. They strap themselves to a long, metal tube-like aircraft the size of one end of a football field and weighing more than a hundred tons. Each passenger will spend the duration of the flight looking only into the rear of the seat in front of them. They are not able to see where they are going or where they have been. They place their lives in the hands of pilots and crew they have never met, and they trust them to carry them to heights of thirty-five thousand feet to deliver them safely to their destination. Now that, my friend, is faith.

A conversation with an airline pilot really landed the concept and brought the whole faith-walk lifestyle out of the fog and into focus for me. I believe it will for you, too.

I have often wondered how airline pilots operate their aircraft, particularly in inclement weather. Recently I had a conversation with Eric, an airline pilot who just retired from flying commercial and military airplanes for more than thirty years. A wise Christian man, Eric gave me a great deal of insight concerning what goes on in the cockpit of an aircraft. I was amazed to hear what my friend had to say.

Eric describes the experience of flying an aircraft this way: "There is great potential for your body and your emotions to play tricks on you. They may actually lie to you, sending information to your brain that is not necessarily true. While flying in fog or bad weather when visibility is poor—*in the soup,* in pilot jargon—it is possible for your body to experience a sense of unsteadiness. This condition is called *vertigo* or *spatial disorientation.* This happens when a malfunction in the inner ear occurs, leaving a pilot in a state of confusion. In laymen's terms, this means you think you know which end is up—but you're wrong. In some cases, your body will tell you that you are flying right side up, when in actuality you could be flying upside down!"

Eric said that airline pilots are trained repeatedly not to

listen to their bodies or rely on their emotions. They are trained to trust, to put complete faith in the aircraft's instrument panel. In all flying conditions—on clear days and, predominantly, when the pilot is flying in bad weather—the pilot is trained to scan the instrument panel. The information on the instrument panel will tell him how to fly the airplane safely. He checks and cross-checks between the altitude gyro, the altimeter, the airspeed indicator and other sophisticated instruments to gather conclusive information about airspeed, altitude, the position of the aircraft and other pertinent details. Each instrument coordinates with all the others. Even if one instrument fails, the pilot is trained to accommodate for it. *Rule number one: Trust the instruments.*

Eric told me that a pilot must spend countless hours in training before he ever enters a real aircraft. He must commit himself to countless hours of strict training, where he will learn how every instrument inside the aircraft's cockpit functions before he ever leaves the ground. In a controlled environment, he will fly under circumstances simulating all kinds of conditions without ever leaving the ground. If a pilot is trained to fly 757s, he cannot fly MD-88s. Pilots are only permitted to fly the aircraft on which they have been trained. If you desire to be a good pilot, then you must read and know how to operate your aircraft under all flying conditions. *Rule number two: Study the manual.*

Air Traffic Control is watching the craft at all times on a sophisticated screen and giving the pilot critical information and instructions regarding the takeoff, cruising and landing of the aircraft. A pilot may be requested to make an increase or decrease in airspeed, change altitude or observe some other instructions. It is imperative that the pilot comply with these requests, or he risks jamming up the works. His decisions will always affect others. *Rule number three: Obey the commands from Air Traffic Control.*

Eric is a Sunday school teacher in his home church. He gave me one of the finest lessons I've ever been taught. He asked me, "When life gets tough, and you find yourself in a personal fog, will you be led by your emotions literally to fly by the seat of your pants, or will you trust the facts?" Learn to check and cross-check your faith walk. Do you have a strong and vibrant relationship with Jesus Christ? Do you have a strong church fellowship where your personal spiritual growth can be realized? Are you maximizing your spiritual potential, using your gifts and talents with a great sense of purpose? Do you have accountability partners who will be honest enough to tell you when you are headed in the wrong direction? Even if you are weak in one area, the strength of your faith walk will accommodate for those weak areas. This is what it really means to walk by faith, not by sight. If you don't trust the facts of your faith, disaster is certain.

Eric asked me if I made it a habit to study the manual—the Bible. Do I exercise what the manual has taught me? No one in his right mind would try to fly an airplane without first reading the manual. Then why do so many people try to live life without reading God's instruction manual? You need training, purpose and direction. You need someone to lead you along to help you discover truth and apply it to your life. Lean on the Lord to help you understand the Bible, God's instruction manual for life.

Eric drove home my personal lesson concerning faith with this last point. He reminded me always to listen for instruction from the Holy Spirit, who is the believer's Air Traffic Controller. He is watching how I live at all times, and He is giving me daily guidance on each direction that I should take. If I am disobedient, then my actions will command a reaction. First my disobedience will affect me. My failure to obey will affect those who are closest to me, my family and other loved ones.

Sin has a ripple effect. Before long, one act of disobedience could affect countless lives. If I am obedient, though, I will reach my destination safely. Others who accompany me on the journey will enjoy the ride as well. Developing a keen ear that is bent toward the Holy Spirit's instruction will afford me many rewarding moments on my journey of faith, allowing me to reach my destination.

Has this ever happened to you? One moment you believe God for the impossible. The next, you are drowning in a sea of doubt, controlled by your feelings. The bottom line of faith is summed up in simple terms. Believe it before you see it. Faith is your positive response to what God has said. When a heart is full of faith, it will always do what it takes to dispel doubt and fear. It will always go to extreme measures. So, you have to go with what you know—not by what you feel. You will be reminded of this important fact throughout this book, because so many people are living by feelings. Faith comes by hearing the Word of God. So, the more you *hear*, the more you *know*. The Scriptures will equip you to fight against the enemy's weapon of doubt.

Read the parable of the sower in Mark chapter 4. Jesus said that the cares of this world will choke out the word that is in your heart, causing it to be unfruitful (Mark 4:18–19). Your faith and God's Word go hand in hand. That means if you allow the enemy to choke out God's promises, your faith will begin to dry up with it. When that happens, you are sure to falter in your walk. To prevent this, you must starve your doubts by feeding your faith a steady diet of the Word of God. Keep your eyes on Jesus—not on your circumstances…not on yourself…but on Jesus.

Walking by faith is hard work. Like building a house with a

hammer and nails, it will mean being bumped and bruised. It will require sweat equity. You will shed tears of disappointment. You will even have to tear down some things and start over again. It will demand that you throw off anything that threatens you and your relationship with Christ. But with the help of the Holy Spirit, you will be able to run the Christian race with patience. Keeping your eyes on Jesus, the One in whom we place our faith, is the most important thing.

> Therefore, since we are surrounded by such a great cloud of witnesses, let us throw off everything that hinders and the sin that so easily entangles, and let us run with perseverance the race marked out for us. Let us fix our eyes on Jesus, the author and perfecter of our faith.
>
> —HEBREWS 12:1–2

Faith is your positive response to what God has said.

We don't live in a perfect world. Far from it. Sometimes things won't go as you think they should. That is when trusting in God's sovereignty is essential. Even the giants of our faith failed. But they are called *giants* because they picked themselves up, dusted themselves off and went on to complete their missions. You can be a champion of faith too if you always keep Jesus in view. You can speak faith to the issues in your life. You will sing praises to God in the face of your enemies and walk on top of the deep waters of doubt.

A great author and theologian of the church by the name of Charles H. Spurgeon once wrote some words that inspired me to write a song called *Trust His Heart*. I think his words say it best.

> God is too wise to be mistaken. God is too good to be unkind. And when you can't trace His hand, trust His heart.

For the kingdom of God is not a matter of talk but of power.

—1 CORINTHIANS 4:20

CHAPTER 2

Passing Your *Faith* Along

W HILE STROLLING ALONG Main Street in a beautiful North Georgia mountain town, I decided to step in and browse around an antique store. The proprietor greeted me and asked me how I was doing. I said with a smile, "Excellent, and getting better!"

She raised her eyebrows with curiosity and said, "Wow, you're so happy. What's your sign?"

"Well," I answered, "my sign is the sign of the cross of Christ!"

"Really?" she said. "What difference does that make?"

"It makes all the difference in the world," I told her. "I can know for sure that God loves me and has a plan for my life. No matter what I'm going through, everything is going to work out for my best. In spite of all the stuff that's going on, it's a wonderful life." She had a look of amazement in her eyes. As I wrote a check for my purchases, I invited her to give Jesus a try. She said she'd think about it.

I wished her a good day and left the store, only to be followed out to the sidewalk by a young gentleman who must have been eavesdropping on our conversation. "I can tell that you know how to talk to God," he said to me. "Would you pray for me?"

I took his hands in mine, and right there on the sidewalk in front of the store, I prayed for him. When I opened my eyes, I saw tears welling up in his. I asked him if he had a relationship with God. "No, not really," he responded. I asked him if he'd like to begin one, and he said yes. We prayed, and the young man asked Jesus into his heart right there on Main Street in a little North Georgia mountain town.

God used a simple conversation in an antique store to whet the appetite of a spiritually hungry young man who wanted something more than the world had to offer. The sails of my faith rose a little higher that day as they were caught up by the gentle wind of the Holy Spirit's presence. It elevated my faith to share Christ with someone who needed to know Him.

Sharing one's love for Christ with others who don't know Him is easy if you just meet them right where they live.

I recently visited a church for a Sunday evening concert. After the concert, we talked about the joy that we get from sharing our faith. The music minister stated that each Sunday morning as the church staff gathers to pray for the Sunday services, they go around the room and share stories about the people with which each person has shared the gospel that week. He said a big part of sharing his faith is done in small acts.

One week he shared a word of encouragement with a waitress in a local restaurant, and then left her a good tip for her service. Another time, he made one high school student's day by going to watch him play baseball. Then he gave him a ride home after the game.

Sharing one's love for Christ with others who don't know Him is easy if you just meet them right where they live. It's like giving an umbrella to a man standing in the pouring rain. It's like giving food to the hungry and water to the thirsty. We are commanded to reach out beyond ourselves to change the world around us.

Lost people can tell instantly if you care. They will know if you're for real. And they will know if you believe what you're talking about. In other words, people can tell if you're talking loud but saying nothing. Real faith has its finger on the pulse of the needs of people. *God requires that we have a faith that motivates the heart. We must have a faith that is touchable.* Our faith should compel us to move out of our comfort zones.

WALKING THE WALK OF FAITH

Has the Holy Spirit ever impressed upon you that you might be talking the talk of faith but not walking the walk of faith? Have you ever been so absorbed in your own busyness, even your own ministry, that you ignored the needs of those around you? You may have even taken pride in the accomplishments of your Christian work, but in actuality you may not be seeing very many lives changed.

If we are not careful, we will miss our opportunities to seize the moment. It's easy to talk about faith. It's another thing to put faith into action. Jesus reached out to people with such a heart of deep compassion. He exhibited true care and concern. Then He was moved to act. God continues to show me that people are desperate, lost and without purpose apart from

Him. He is turning this heart of mine inside out with a passion for Him and a compassion for people.

Numerous times in Matthew's Gospel, the Scriptures capture Christ's care for the people around Him. *"He was moved with compassion…"* He was moved. Then He was compelled to act. I believe these are the key ingredients that keep a heart tender and eager to share who Christ is and what He can do to change a life. The needs of people are so apparent that we don't have to look very far to find an opportunity to share the life-changing power of Christ's love with others. Developing an acute awareness of the dire needs of people is often the tenderizer that moves our hearts from the state of apathy to the state of action.

THE CALL FOR COMPASSION

One vivid memory shook me out of my comfortable stupor. I don't believe I'll ever forget it. It was in the mid-1980s, during the early days of our music ministry. I had been asked to come to Fort Lauderdale, Florida, to sing at a large music conference. Up to that point I had not traveled far from home to minister. So I was extremely excited when the host church invited me to come and sing at the conference and offered to pay for two airfares so Charles could go along.

Upon our arrival at the airport in Florida, we found that the host church had sent a chauffeur-driven limousine to pick us up. We thought we had just been crowned the king and queen of the world. We had never ridden in a limousine before. (It didn't enter our minds that it was probably more convenient and more cost effective to our host to employ a limo service to transport their guests for huge conferences like the one we were attending.) Charles and I giggled as we crawled into the back of the stretch vehicle and eased into the black leather seats.

Like kids in a candy store, our eyes widened as we passed the luxurious yachts parked along the marinas. As we pulled onto the brick-covered drive of the hotel, we tried counting the floors to the high-rise building. We looked at each other without saying a word, but inside we were saying, "We could certainly get used to this kind of treatment."

I glanced at the uniformed doorman in the distance, but suddenly something caught my eye. I turned to look, and there, nestled beneath the beautiful and expensive landscaping, a homeless man was asleep on a cardboard box. For a moment, my mind was confused. *How could this be? This is so out of place.* In the midst of all that luxury and decadence lay a man, hidden in the bushes, gripping a bag that probably contained all of his worldly possessions.

I knew that inside the walls of that grand hotel were hundreds of soft beds with down pillows, soap with running water and enough food and drink to feed an army. I suddenly felt sick and empty. I quickly checked us in to our hotel room and took a walk out to where the man had made his temporary home. But he was gone. Just that quickly someone had discovered him lying there and shooed him off the property like a stray animal.

Faith is something to be given away. It is something to be shared.

My heart sank as I walked back to our room. While I walked, I prayed for that man. Wherever he was, I prayed that God would use someone to lift him up and out of his pit of despair.

Then I prayed for me, that God would bring me down to a place of humility. I prayed that God would never let me be so comfortable, so well-to-do, so full of food or so full of myself that I become blinded to the needs of others.

A few days later, I wrote the words to this song.

> Show me how to love
> In the true meaning
> Of the word
> Teach me to sacrifice
> Expecting nothing in return
> I want to give my life away
> Becoming more like You
> Each and every day
> My words are not enough
> Show me how to love.[1]

That incident moved me to another level of compassion. But it also created in me a sense of urgency. Seeing that man in that condition broke my heart. Because I tried to help the man but didn't reach him in time, I became determined from then on to love the unlovable and touch the untouchable, to let my actions speak louder than words.

Faith is a verb. Faith is an action word. Faith is something to be given away. It is something to be shared. And when it is shared, it will stir up more faith in the one who gives. The faith of the one on the receiving end will be stirred as well. Faith is a living and active gift that always anticipates what God will do to bring about a favorable end.

Catherine Booth, the cofounder of The Salvation Army, said, "Where there is real faith there is always expectation."[2] No matter how small your faith is, God can use you to bring about change. *God requires that we have a faith that activates our hands. We must have a faith that is tangible.* We must not only talk about how much we love God and people; we must do something about it.

We have the misconception that God can only be moved by the faith of those who are pastors or those on television or people with large public ministries. But the Bible demonstrates over and over again that God always uses the simplest things— what little we hold in our hand—to accomplish His work. And when His work is accomplished, it will be obvious to you and to others that it will have been the hand of God that did it.

> *The most unlearned person with a passionate faith is more believable than the most articulate person without it.*

In Matthew 9:22, Jesus healed a woman who had been bleeding for twelve long years. In Matthew 9:29, Jesus healed two blind men. In both of these situations…to both of these desperate, hopeless people, Jesus said, "*Your* faith has made you whole." No matter who you are or what your circumstances may be, never be persuaded that God will not recognize *your* faith. The most unlearned person with a passionate faith is more believable than the most articulate person without it.

LITTLE IS MUCH WITH GOD

The sixth chapter of John gives a profound example of how

God takes the little things, even the ridiculous, to perform the miraculous.

> When Jesus looked up and saw a great crowd coming toward him, he said to Philip, "Where shall we buy bread for these people to eat?" He asked this only to test him, for he already had in mind what he was going to do.
>
> Philip answered him, "Eight months' wages would not buy enough bread for each one to have a bite!"
>
> Another of his disciples, Andrew, Simon Peter's brother, spoke up, "Here is a boy with five small barley loaves and two small fish, but how far will they go among so many?"
>
> Jesus said, "Have the people sit down." There was plenty of grass in that place, and the men sat down, about five thousand of them. Jesus then took the loaves, gave thanks, and distributed to those who were seated as much as they wanted. He did the same with the fish.
>
> When they had all had enough to eat, he said to his disciples, "Gather the pieces that are left over. Let nothing be wasted." So they gathered them and filled twelve baskets with the pieces of the five barley loaves left over by those who had eaten.
>
> —JOHN 6:5–13

Truly, little is much when God is in it. In the materialistic culture in which we live, we often believe that money is the answer to every problem. We've been conditioned to think that if we give a big enough check to the missions campaign, we have done our part. All the money in the world cannot reach people for Christ by itself. People reach people for Christ. When God wants to show Himself strong, He prefers to use simple things. The disciples realized that even if they pooled all their resources together, they still would not be able to produce enough food to feed such a large crowd.

This impossible situation was a perfect setup for God to do what only He could do through them. He used a common little boy, a plain lunch—two fish, five loaves—and simple disciples to accomplish one of the most magnificent miracles recorded in the Bible. (I once heard a speaker call the twelve, in reference to their simplicity, the "duh-ciples.")

BE AVAILABLE

For God to use you, you don't have to be *able*, just *available*. You don't have to be the strongest, the prettiest, the brightest or the most affluent. God often uses those with what we consider lesser gifts to do more, and those with what we think are greater gifts to do less. The very thing that you think is unacceptable is the very thing that God will use to bring about the miraculous and advance His cause.

Maybe you think God couldn't use you because of your age, gender or race. You may think that you are unacceptable because of your sinful past. We see God at His best when He uses unlikely people who have the odds stacked against them. What we could never do in the natural, God does in the supernatural.

> *For God to use you, you don't have to be able, just available.*

You see, when faith is involved, you don't need an overabundance of things in your hand. Simple things, even simple people, will do.

☕ A little boy named David slew a great big giant named Goliath with a sling and a stone (1 Sam. 17).

☕ God used Moses, a man with a speech impediment, to lead an entire nation of people to the Promised Land (Exod. 13).

☕ God defied the laws of nature to bless two senior citizens, the father of faith, Abraham, at one hundred years old, and his wife, Sarah, at ninety, to become first-time parents (Gen. 21).

☕ God caused Gideon and a mere three hundred fighting men to confuse and defeat thousands of Midianites without even drawing a weapon (Judg. 7).

☕ God greatly used Rahab, a known prostitute in the city of Jericho and one who was rejected by society. Rahab hid two spies in her home. These men were on a mission from God (Josh. 2).

☕ God used a man by the name of Paul, who hated the early church and persecuted Christians because of their faith. After his conversion, God used the apostle Paul to carry the message of the gospel, not only to the Jews but also to the Gentiles (Acts 9).

☕ God chose an unwed, teenage girl to be the mother of our Lord and Savior, Jesus Christ (Luke 1).

Isn't it just like God to use the broken, the young, the aged, the poor, male, female, the unappealing, the rejected, the weak, the small and the otherwise unacceptable as servants in His great kingdom? They were all simple. But they were all willing to be used to be a display of God's power.

God not only requires that we have a faith that is touchable and tangible, but He also desires that we have the knowledge to back it up. *He requires that we have a faith that obligates the head. We must have a faith that is teachable.* Proverbs 10:14 says, "Wise men store up knowledge." In Proverbs 2:9–10, we read, "Then you will understand what is right and just and fair—every good path. For wisdom will enter your heart, and knowledge will be pleasant to your soul."

Equip yourself to meet the needs of people. Let me be the first to admit that it seems that the more I learn, the more I realize I don't know. After going to school for sixteen years and teaching school at the middle high and college level for twelve years combined, the greatest lesson I've learned is that I still have a lot to learn. I can't even say that I have begun to exhaust the knowledge of the things I claim to know a lot about. I have only begun to touch the surface of what there is to know about music or language. I have been a student of the Bible for most of my life. But I have yet to dig deep enough to land at the bottom of the vast truths of God's Word. I will study God's Word voraciously until the day I die—and never come to the end of it all. The more I know, I realize the more I need to know. I believe God honors that kind of faith.

> *God requires that we have a faith that obligates the head.*

We should have such an appetite for the Word of God that we are willing to dig deep to find the truths that will transform our lives. Paul wrote:

...Christ, in whom are hidden all the treasures of wisdom and knowledge.

—COLOSSIANS 2:2–3

Paul dedicated his life to the work of the gospel. He was delighted when he saw believers with a firm faith and a thirst to know more of Christ.

More and more, I anticipate uncovering what I don't know about God. But I also rejoice over what I do know about Him. I gave myself an assignment, one that I encourage you to practice as well. I began to make a list of the things that I *know* about God. I've listed a few of them below.

THINGS I KNOW ABOUT GOD

- I *know* the Word of God is true—John 1:1.

- I *know* God loves me—John 3:16.

- I *know* God has a plan for my life—Jeremiah 29:11.

- I *know* God has ordained every one of my steps—Psalm 139:16.

- I *know* that everything, the good, the bad and the ugly, will work together for my best—Romans 8:28.

- I *know* that God's power is greater than that of the devil—1 John 4:4.

- I *know* that God owns everything—Psalm 24:1.

- I *know* that every one of my needs are met—Philippians 4:19.

- I *know* that I am able to accomplish the work that God has assigned for me to do—Philippians 4:13.

> I *know* that absolutely nothing can come between me and God's love for me—Romans 8:38–39.

> I *know* that Christ was crucified and died on a cruel cross as a sacrifice for sin—Matthew 27:50.

> And I *know* that He is coming again soon to catch believers up in the clouds to reign with Him forever—1 Thessalonians 4:16–18.

I could go on and on with the little that I know and still just scratch the surface. Time and space won't permit me to continue with the assignment here. I'll continue to add to my list later, and you can, too. I realize I don't know it all, but what I do know truly bolsters my faith.

The Christian must keep the faith—but not to himself.

Yes, faith is a verb. It's an action word. Remember that faith *motivates* our heart. We must be touchable. A heart of compassion will keep us out of our comfort zone, and the fire of compassion will always burn away complacency. Remember that faith *activates* our hands. We must be tangible and willing to pass our faith along. Words are not enough. The Christian must keep the faith—but not to himself. Faith *obligates* our head. We must be teachable, adding knowledge to our acts of worship and work. Real students of God's Word don't merely gargle at the fountain. They pause to drink deeply.

Mature believers let their actions speak louder than their

words. Remember 1 Corinthians 4:20:

> For the kingdom of God is not a matter of talk but of power.

Is your faith passive, or is it actively working in your life? Step out into deeper waters, and trust God to do the impossible in you, with you, through you and for you.

Be completely humble and gentle; be patient, bearing with one another in love. Make every effort to keep the unity of the Spirit through the bond of peace. There is one body and one Spirit—just as you were called to one hope when you were called—one Lord, one faith, one baptism; one God and Father of all, who is over all and through all and in all.

—EPHESIANS 4:2–6

CHAPTER 3

The Fellowship
of *Faith*

OR ME, IT was a privilege to grow up as a preacher's
daughter. As a preacher's kid in a small town, life had its
share of pressures. But now that I have raised children of my
own, I pray that I have passed on to them the godly heritage
that was given to me. My father was the pastor of a thriving
church in Jackson, Michigan. He, the late Reverend Willie G.
Wade, and my mother, Mrs. Georgie Wade, served together at
the Lily Missionary Baptist Church for just short of forty years.
It was the first and only church they served.

My parents expected my sister, my brothers and me to be in
church and to find a place to serve. By age nine, I had the
responsibility of church pianist. For a grade school girl, this
was quite a workload. I played the piano for three choirs. That
meant I was required to be at three rehearsals a week.

Occasionally, our church was invited to other fellowships
during the week. Our choir, or a good contingency of members, would accompany the pastor and church members to
support the effort. I was expected to be there too, even if it
meant going out of town on a school night. I was always a good
student, and it never seemed to hurt my studies.

Then there was Sunday. Our church delivered a live radio

broadcast early every Sunday morning—rain or shine, snow or sleet. The broadcast was followed by Sunday school, which was followed by the morning worship service. Then there was an afternoon service. Then an evening service followed that. The schedule was rather demanding for the average church member, let alone a youngster, but God in His great big plan knew that those years would be on-the-job training for the ministry He would entrust to me today.

Although our church was a vibrant and growing one, there was no full-time staff. Dad worked a full-time job during the day and pastored our congregation of about three hundred fifty members. In the eyes of a nine-year-old in a small town, this was a mega-church. Church staff, for the most part, volunteered their services or received a small stipend. Our church was warm and exciting with colorful members that still make my memory come alive with details.

One of the choirs that I accompanied was appropriately called the Junior Choir. If you were in grade school, whether you could sing or not, you were expected to be a member. I recall our youth choir director, Reverend Earl Harden, an older gentlemen—but he had the energy of a teenager. Always well dressed and impeccably groomed, Reverend Harden would meet us at rehearsal with an attitude of contagious enthusiasm. Before our rehearsal time, we'd spend some time warming up. There were no la-la-la's or singing the notes on the scale for us. We had our own cheers. We'd yell loudly enough to make any voice teacher cringe. We'd shout to the tops of our lungs. You would have thought you were at a pep rally. And when we sang, we sang with the same attitude. In our estimation, if it wasn't loud, it wasn't singing.

Although our church had hymnals, we only used them to read the Responsive Reading and the Church Covenant. We rarely used the hymnal for singing. It's impossible to clap your hands while holding a hymnal. I am grateful to God that my church had the patience to endure the piano playing of a nine-year-old who was learning to play by ear. Early on, I could only play in one key. That was the key of C. They sang in the key of C for a very long time. No matter whether the key was too high or too low—it was too bad; they continued to sing that song in the key of C. But I kept showing up, and God kept blessing my abilities. Pretty soon I was comfortable at playing in just about any key. Truly, little is much when God is in it.

That's what I loved about growing up in our church. My father encouraged the church members to use whatever gift they had. If you could sing, although you may not have been the best, you were encouraged to sing as if you were Mahalia Jackson. If you could teach, even though you may not have won any awards, you were encouraged to teach.

I have always loved the church. I love the message of the church, for the gospel was and still is the reason for our existence. I love the music of the church. Its rhythm and repetition could make you forget you ever had a problem. I love the people of the church with their character and colorful personalities.

The members were dedicated to the life flow of the church. In the winter, they pressed their way to worship through snow and ice. Even when the temperatures dipped down around zero degrees, most members didn't let that deter them. In the summer we had no air conditioning, so the men wiped their brows with white handkerchiefs while the women and children moved the hot air around with fans that advertised the local funeral home on the back.

I'll never forget the way that Daddy cared for his flock of members. He had a contagious passion for the Bible. He taught it thoroughly and with ease at Wednesday night Bible study, and he preached with fervor every Sunday. The pictures in my mind roll by like home movies.

Every Sunday morning the members would come to the church decked out in their Sunday best. Most of the members were in the sanctuary by 11 A.M., but it was not an uncommon thing for latecomers to be fifteen to twenty minutes late. We all knew we would be there for a while, so they didn't see any harm in arriving a few minutes late.

There would be singing, Scripture reading, prayer, some testimonies and an offering. The church clerk would read the announcements. Then we'd have some more singing, prayer, some more testimonies, and we'd raise another offering. Just before the sermon, the choir would sing another soul-stirring selection that would bring the congregation to its feet.

Then, gracing the pulpit donned in his black robe and carrying his worn-out Bible, Daddy would read his text for the morning. He would expound on each verse, building a foundation like a brick mason. The congregation hung on every word, urging him on with their shouts of *amen*. With the organist mimicking every phrase he preached, it wouldn't be long before Daddy would catch hold of a tune—preaching the sermon in a singing style. As Daddy went up, the congregation went up with him. Before long, the entire church was caught up and carried away with the spirit. The Holy Spirit's conviction brought men, women, boys and girls to the altar to accept Christ as their personal Savior. I remember walking down the aisle to the altar one Sunday morning as an eight-year-old girl. My father led me to Jesus, and the church members welcomed me with the right hand of fellowship. Each Sunday the worship service lasted about two and a half to three hours.

After graduation from high school and the local junior college, I went on to Spring Arbor College, now Spring Arbor University, which is just outside my hometown. Spring Arbor is a predominantly white Christian college affiliated with the

Free Methodist Church. Needless to say, the entire worship experience was different from what I'd ever known. Everyone was in the sanctuary promptly at 11 A.M. Everyone held a hymnal, so no one clapped his or her hands. Besides, it's next to impossible to clap to "A mighty fortress is our God, a bulwark never failing…"[1]

They raised only one offering. Everyone quietly read the announcements that were printed in the church bulletin. The choir sang softly, and only one song. No one said *amen*. After the pastor's lecture, the church service was dismissed—precisely one hour after it started. But for the first time in a long time, I could sit there in the pew and not be preoccupied with what I was going to play for the invitational hymn. I hung on to every word of the sermon. Although the worship service was vastly different, I heard the same gospel message, and the Holy Spirit ministered profoundly to my heart in ways that altered the course of my life.

> *The truth is a lot like peanut butter—substantial and rich in nutrients.*

PEANUT BUTTER AND JELLY SANDWICHES

I have always been fascinated by the different qualities the body of Christ brings to the family of God. Each culture, particularly as it pertains to blacks and whites, has so much to contribute. We have a tendency to think that one race or culture has more to contribute than the other. But I have found that we all bring something unique to the worship experience.

In an effort to demonstrate that uniqueness, I am going to give you an illustration. Forgive me if it appears elementary. Just work with me for a moment.

I have often likened the body of Christ to a peanut butter and jelly sandwich. Historically, most pastors and preachers of conservative white churches have been exposed to Christian education. In the finest seminaries money could buy, they were exposed to the fundamental truths of the Christian faith. These preachers dedicated years to the study and the preaching of these foundational truths.

The truth is a lot like peanut butter—substantial and rich in nutrients. It's packed full of vitamins and minerals. If you were stranded on a desert island and had to eat peanut butter for the rest of your life, you could survive. But peanut butter, like truth, is thick and dry. It sticks to the roof of your mouth, and it's awfully hard to swallow. Some have even been known to choke on it. That's a lot like some Sunday worship services in some conservative white churches. Typically, white churches have had a lot of truth but very little spirit. Worship services like that need some sweetening up.

Historically, most black pastors and preachers did not go to seminary. Because of segregation, discrimination or economics, black people could not attend these seminaries and universities. Many blacks in the Old South could not read or write. So they gathered as much information as they could, interpreting it as best as they could. Since the days of slavery, black people have fought to rise above the social, economic and racial conditions in America. Before the twentieth century, the black man could not vote, go to school or live or work wherever he wished. For the most part, the only institution that he could call his very own was the church. Church was where he could find emotional release from the harsh realities of life. In the church, black people were free to sing, shout, dance and respond to the preaching with no inhibitions.

Most black churches had lots of spirit. This spirit added the element of joy to the worship service. Joy in the spirit is a lot like jelly. It's sweet and feels real good going down. The music, the singing and the emotional preaching is enough to make a parishioner shout right out of his shoes. However, it's not healthy to consume jelly in large doses. It may upset your stomach and could cause cavities in your teeth. So often, as high-spirited as it was, this Sunday morning experience did not have enough substance to strengthen most churchgoers long enough to get to the Wednesday night service. It lacked substance. Historically, black churches have had a lot of spirit, but they didn't have access to the truth.

Peanut butter alone will leave you lacking. Jelly by itself won't satisfy for long. But if you combine the two ingredients, the peanut butter and the jelly, you have the beginnings of a good meal. The substance of the peanut butter and the sweetening of the jelly balance each other beautifully.

But even though peanut butter and jelly are a perfect blend, these two ingredients are nothing without fresh-baked, wholesome, whole-wheat bread. Who is the Bread of Life? In John 6:35, Jesus said, "I am the bread of life. He who comes to me will never go hungry."

Our deepest longing is for bread. Not only the kind of bread that you buy at the grocery store, but bread that is heaven sent. Bread is the most basic of foods. As a matter of fact, bread is the foundation of the food pyramid. The *World Book Encyclopedia* confirms that bread is the most widely eaten food. It provides a larger share of our body's energy and protein than any other food. As a matter of fact, whole-wheat bread provides almost all of the natural vitamins and minerals that we need. On top of all that, whole-wheat bread is high in fiber. There is nothing that is more satisfying than fresh bread. Have you ever risen in the morning to the smell of fresh-baked bread? If you want to make your house warm and inviting, or if you want to make somebody feel welcome in your neighborhood, just bake some bread.

Jesus Christ is the Bread of Life. He is the only one who is able to satisfy your hunger. Jesus satisfies every spiritual need. He fulfills every spiritual longing, and He meets every spiritual requirement. This Living Bread leaves nothing out. His blessings are never stale. His mercies are never left over from yesterday.

> [His mercies] are new every morning;
>   great is your faithfulness.
>
> —LAMENTATIONS 3:23

Jesus is all you need to be truly satisfied. It's not Jesus plus money or Jesus plus ambition or Jesus plus education or Jesus plus your spouse. It's not Jesus plus anything. It's Jesus *plus nothing*. Jesus is enough all by Himself. Is it any wonder that it is said that bread is the poor man's food? Anybody can afford spiritual bread because it's free, and it's always available. There's always an abundant supply. Jesus invites all who are hungry to come and eat. Anyone who is longing, yearning for significance and purpose, is welcome to come and dine at the Master's table.

The peanut butter and jelly sandwich is a simple way to demonstrate the need for both spirit and truth in the church. If you take the substance of truth, add to that the joy of the Spirit and serve the message of Jesus to a hungry and dying world, people will eat and be satisfied. If the body of Christ is to be whole, it is essential that the church have both qualities to offer a hungry world. It is not a case of spirit *or* truth. Both spirit *and* truth are essential.

> God is spirit, and his worshipers must worship in spirit
> and in truth.
>
> —JOHN 4:24

This is a good thing to remember. Operate in the spirit without the truth, and you blow up. Expound on the truth without the spirit, and you dry up. But when the spirit and the truth walk hand in hand, you grow up.

If you take the substance of truth, add to that the joy of the Spirit and serve Jesus to a hungry and dying world, people will eat and be satisfied.

I love the body of Christ, and I am encouraged by what I see. Black churches enjoy hearing the truths of God's Word preached in their churches now more than ever before. More and more, white churches are experiencing the joy that only the Spirit of God can bring. As the body of Christ comes together to worship in unity, we give each other permission to express ourselves in different ways.

Black believers give their white sisters and brothers permission to enjoy themselves in the worship service, to say *amen* and wave their hands in agreement. I sang an up-tempo praise song in a white church recently, and the worshipers were so over-come with joy that they formed a line and danced all up and down the aisles. White believers give black sisters and brothers permission to be quiet and reflective. While attending a black church one Sunday morning, during a quiet and prayerful moment, the Holy Spirit moved so sweetly across the sanctuary. One by one, worshipers made their way to the altar to pray.

Little by little, we are coming together down here. And coming together down here is imperative if we plan to spend eternity together in heaven. We have come a long way as a body of believers. But we still have a long way to go. I heard someone say that there is not an institution in America that has more visibility and less influence than the church. Whether you agree with that statement or not, one thing is true. There is still a lot of work to do.

LEARN TO BE A SERVANT

A love for the church and the body of Christ has carried me around the world. I once sang on a Christian cruise that sailed to Alaska. That great state keeps me in awe. Everything about Alaska is grand. I've always said, "When God created Alaska, He was showing off." The big sky is above you. The vast ocean is beneath you. The majestic mountains are on the horizon. Then to that, add whales, eagles, fishing and glaciers. Like I said, "When God made Alaska, He was showing off."

On the day that our ship pulled into Glacier Bay, I was amazed. The glaciers stood there in front of me—millions of years old. Compressed ice mountains stood on display, a gem-like shade of crystal blue. Every so often, the glaciers broke off in huge chunks and crashed down into the water.

I sat in my seat reading my Bible:

> Come and see what God has done,
> how awesome his works in man's behalf!
> He turned the sea into dry land,
> they passed through the waters on foot—
> come, let us rejoice in him.
>
> —PSALM 66:5–6

Then I read, "The fool says in his heart, 'There is no God'" (Ps. 53:1). I read more:

> God is our refuge and strength,
> an ever-present help in trouble.
> Therefore we will not fear, though the earth give way
> and the mountains fall into the heart of the sea,
> though its waters roar and foam
> and the mountains quake with their surging.
>
> —PSALM 46:1–3

As I sat there watching the words from the Bible come to life before my eyes, the drink steward, a young Filipino man, stopped at my seat and remarked with delight, "The Bible... the Word of God...It's my favorite Book in the whole world." He proceeded to speak of his deep, sweet faith in Christ. He was happy to have Christians on board the ship for the week. His eyes grew tender when he said that even though he was working, he worshiped with us during our worship services. He told me of the crew's worship service that convened there on the ship. He asked me to spread the word and extended an invitation for the other guest speakers and musicians and myself to be guests at the crew's weekly worship service. He explained that because the crew had to meet for worship after their work was finished, their scheduled weekly worship hour was 12:30 A.M.

Groggy-eyed and sleep deprived, four of us, all Christian women, two of us black and two of us white, met with eight

Christian brothers from the Philippines. I believe that although we were a small band, we were mighty in God's eyes. We sang together. We prayed together. We shared insights from God's Word. We rejoiced together. Although there are issues in the United States that divided us as black and white Americans, we were then, and we are now, unified by the Spirit of Christ, and we sensed that unity in the worship service. There are foreign policies that separate us as nations, but in that meeting room in the early hours of the morning, we knew we were one body of believers, worshiping God in spirit and in truth. We realized that God did not place us here to see through each other but to see each other through.

God allows us the privilege of worshiping under one flag—the banner of love. I once heard someone say, "We may have come over here on different ships, but we're all in the same boat now." That is what fellowship is—a collection of fellows in the same ship. We must all push together, pull together, row together, sink or swim together. If you rejoice, I rejoice with you. If you grieve, I grieve with you. If you fall down, I lift you up.

God did not place us here to see through each other but to see each other through.

Do you believe that as sisters in Christ, we all have that same goal in mind? If you are truly my sister in Christ, then I know you agree, because that's what the Bible demonstrates. So I'll hold up one side of the bloodstained banner, and you hold up the other. Together we will endeavor to worship one Lord, to walk in one faith, to wade into the cleansing waters of one baptism, to love one God who is Lord over all, who lives in us all and who works through us all.

Faith without works is dead.

—JAMES 2:26, NKJV

CHAPTER 4

Faith

Works

A S A GOSPEL singer and songwriter, I am grateful to God for what I do. It's hard for me to believe that I actually get to live out my dreams. Then I add to that the fact that potentially people can receive a blessing from what I do. God has given me the honor to sing in some of the largest churches in the nation and for conferences, crusades, presidents, prime ministers and kings from all over the world. On the other hand, it has been my humble privilege to sing in remote villages in East Africa and in prisons for men, women and teenagers here in my own hometown. I've sung at baby dedications, retirement homes for the elderly, weddings and funerals. Whether the audience is young or old, many or few, it is always an honor to share the love of Christ with anybody who will listen.

There's never a dull moment in this life of ministry. Early-morning flights and late-night concerts keep me running at a nonstop pace. A great number of these appearances occur on the weekend, so I have often found myself as a guest in a different church on many Sunday mornings. Because my husband, Charles, travels with me, I try to arrange our hectic schedule to be at our own home church as often as we can get there. Anytime we have a concert on Saturday night and are able to arrange the return flight to get us back home in time for church on Sunday morning, we count it a blessing.

Early one particular Sunday morning, Charles and I were coming in from Florida where I had been in concert the night before. We were physically tired after a short night's sleep and an early morning call to rise and get to the airport. But I was excited, because I'd get to be at our home church. I'd get to sit in the pew and take it all in after giving myself away for days on end without a break. I had anticipated getting to church all weekend long and was so excited when our plane landed at Atlanta's airport right on schedule.

Immediately I began timing all the mundane activities we had to accomplish to get us out of the airport and on the road to church. It wouldn't take too long at all to get our luggage, catch the shuttle to the parking garage, hop in my husband's pickup truck and get to the church on time. But we didn't have a moment to waste.

We were right on schedule as we pulled out of the parking garage and onto the expressway. When we pulled onto the exit nearest our home and our church, Charles noticed that the gas hand on his pickup truck was near empty, so he pulled into the first filling station. We had twenty minutes to spare before the morning worship service began. I was cautious, but not anxious. We'd have to hurry, though. We still would have to find a parking spot and then get good seats. After being away for so long, I wanted to get as close to the front as I could.

Charles pumped the gas and went inside to pay. He walked with a purpose as he headed back toward the truck where I sat counting the minutes. He paused for a moment to allow two young teenage guys to pass in front of him. Their car was in obvious distress, as one tried with all his might to push the dead vehicle and the other tried hard to steer it, with no power steering, into a nearby parking space. Noticing their plight, Charles stepped right in behind the car and delivered some needed and welcomed strength. After the car had come to a resting place in the empty space next to us, Charles nodded his head to their thanks and headed back to our vehicle. I admired my husband's kind generosity. It was nice of him to stop and help, but now it was time to get on to church in a hurry. As Charles opened the door to the driver's side of the truck, he glanced back to see the two young men struggle to raise the car's hood. It was obvious that these kids didn't know the difference between a headlight and the tailpipe.

Without missing a beat, Charles closed the door and headed over to help these two distressed travelers. I looked at the clock on the dashboard. Worship service would start in ten minutes. All Charles had to do was make a quick determination that the car was beyond his ability to help, and we could be on our way. My observation was that the car didn't need repair—it needed a resurrection. I didn't think there was much Charles could do at this point to help them.

Once again, I noted that we were running behind schedule. If we left now, we'd miss the first few songs during praise and worship, but at least I could hear all of the sermon. But after taking a closer look, Charles determined that there was something he could do to help. He went right to it.

I partially rolled down the window on my side of the truck just enough to keep the heat in and the cool spring draft out. I could clearly hear the conversation. As I looked closer, I could see the complexion and the beautiful angular features of the two young men, and I knew instantly they were from Africa. I knew instantly that Charles recognized those features, too. I could tell that he was intrigued by these two strangers. He loves the African nations and goes to Africa at least once annually, sometimes more, to work with the people of Kenya, Uganda and the Congo. With his own hands, he has helped to construct churches, schools and clinics. The friendships that he has established with African Christian brothers there are precious and lifelong.

I heard Charles say something to these two young men about the battery. By now the two young guys were standing back and looking on, keeping their hands warm in their pockets. They could tell that my husband knew what he was doing, and they were not about to get in his way. Charles, like a skilled doctor, made his diagnosis and began the delicate surgery on their ill automobile. He ran to the back of his pickup truck to retrieve the right tools. You can be certain that he had every ratchet, socket and gadget he needed to get the job done. If not, then be certain he could improvise and create it. He's a Johnny-on-the-spot, a Vietnam veteran and a southern country boy who knows how to work his way into and out of most situations.

If he were a contestant on the television show *Survivor*, his opponents would be toast. The man can fix anything and is extremely practical. If your cupboards were bare, he'd be able to make a wonderful meal out of practically nothing. He is the man you want on your losing team or your sinking ship. With Charles in charge, these two young guys from Africa were fortunate, indeed.

Meanwhile, I sat sulking in the truck. Gone was my one opportunity to attend corporate worship. I wouldn't have another opportunity to attend church for several more weeks. My heart sank. I knew I'd never make it to church now. The praise and worship time was over. The pastor would be just about ready to conclude his sermon. I would even miss the offering and the announcements.

Charles had used just about every tool he had to repair the vehicle for these strangers. I heard him instruct one of the guys to hop in and start the car. Without hesitation, the young fellow climbed in and turned the ignition. The sick motor coughed a few times and turned over. With a couple of ferocious pats on the accelerator, the motor began to clear its throat. I glanced over at the young man behind the wheel as he raised his head. His eyes caught mine, and he smiled with pure delight.

It was then that my own eyes were opened. Noticing the delight I saw in that young man's face, I wondered about his story. Where was he from? How did he get to the United States? Where were his parents? Were they here with him or back in Africa? Could he be a refugee fleeing the violence and the ravages of civil war? Could his mother be back home in Africa praying for him at that very moment—praying that when her son is in trouble that some kind and caring Christian man will stop and help him? Could his parents be dead? Could he be a refugee *and* an orphan? Tears welled up in my eyes and compassion gripped my heart as I imagined what could be the story of this young man and his friend. I've been to Africa enough times to know that whatever his story was, it was, no doubt, mingled with pain and loss.

As he slammed the car's hood down fast, I heard Charles give the young men some last words of advice concerning their ailing vehicle. He instructed them like a father. They listened to him like sons. Convicted, I whispered a prayer to God for forgiveness for being cold, callous and selfish. Then I whispered a prayer of thanks to God for a man like Charles who was kind and willing—and that I could call him my own.

When Charles saw the two safely in their car as they backed out of the parking lot, he climbed into his truck and buckled up. I reached over and kissed him on the cheek and told him how much his actions had blessed me. I realized right then and there that I had been to church. I had heard the sermon, complete with several eye-opening illustrations. I had even prayed and responded to my own altar call. I sang softly a verse of a hymn. My heart was full—as full as it had been in many memorable worship services in times past.

Regardless of where you live, you probably don't have to look very far to find someone who could use your help.

REACH OUT TO OTHERS

Almost immediately my mind ran to the parable of the Good Samaritan.

> A man was going down from Jerusalem to Jericho, when he fell into the hands of robbers. They stripped him of his clothes, beat him and went away, leaving him half dead. A priest happened to be going down the same road, and when he saw the man, he passed by on the other side. So too, a Levite, when he came to the place and saw him, passed by on the other side. But a Samaritan, as he traveled, came where the man was; and when he saw him, he took pity on him. He went to him and bandaged his wounds, pouring on oil and wine. Then he put the man on his donkey, took him to an inn and took care of him. The next day he took out two silver coins and gave them to the inn-keeper. "Look

after him," he said, "and when I return, I will reimburse you for any extra expense you may have."

—LUKE 10:30–35

In the parable, the priest and the Levite were religious people who worked in the temple. If you were to compare the priest and the Levite to modern-day, full-time church staff, they would represent the pastor and the music minister. The Bible says that they were "going down" from Jerusalem. So, most likely, they had already been to the temple to perform their religious duties when they saw the wounded man lying alongside the road.

In both cases, the religious men crossed over to the other side of the road, intentionally leaving the beaten man for dead. Maybe they were running late for other religious duties or meetings and didn't have time to stop and care for the man. Maybe they didn't want to get their hands dirty. Maybe they just didn't want to get involved. It could have been that they feared that they would defile themselves and be pronounced ceremonially unclean. Any way you look at it, the wounded man, as far as these religious people were concerned, was on his own.

The Bible defines *our neighbor* as anyone of any race, creed, color or social status who needs our help. Regardless of where you live, you probably don't have to look very far to find someone who could use your help. Too often church people have felt it is their duty to straighten people out, when it is only their responsibility to help people out. In a lot of cases we have left the job of feeding the hungry, clothing the naked and caring for children and widows to the government. We are satisfied with letting our nation's welfare agencies do our part.

In Matthew 25:34, Jesus bestows an inheritance to those who have given the hungry something to eat, the thirsty something to drink, taken care of strangers, clothed the naked, nursed the sick and visited those in prison. He said that if we have done this for people who don't have a voice, for people who go unrecognized and for people whose identities have slipped between the cracks of society, it would be just as if we had done it for the Lord Himself. In other words, we will reap a harvest of blessings if we are personally involved in serving others. Remember, in order for faith to work, we must put it into practice.

The mark of a true Christian is not how good we look sitting in the pew in our church attire on Sunday. It is how well we serve others throughout the week.

A few years ago I was privileged to sing on another Christian cruise, this time to the Bahamas. It was during the month of January, so I didn't mind trading the chilly, winter winds of Georgia for the trade winds, blue skies and tropical waters of the Caribbean. Life aboard the luxury cruise liner was too wonderful for words. Every meal was a culinary experience, featuring delectable delicacies from all over the world. The service provided by the captain and crew was simply impeccable. Our cabin was perfectly maintained and visited by our cabin steward three times a day. Nightly turndown service was complete with chocolates on each bed pillow. At every port, a new sight, a delightful sound and a refreshing experience awaited us. At the end of each excursion we were welcomed back on the ship by cheerful smiles from the crew.

Those who worked on the ship were from all around the world. It was fascinating to hear all the different accents and learn about their families who waited for them back home in their country of origin. As the week progressed, I learned my way around the ship. Several of the porters were Christians and would stop to listen in on my concerts while they worked. I was surprised to notice that the majority of the ship's crew were from other countries besides the United States.

One day, out of curiosity, I asked a porter from the Caribbean a few questions about his working experience aboard the ship. He told me that he made a good living and that he enjoyed seeing the world. I was curious, however, why I hadn't seen a relative number of Americans working aboard the ship. His words stung me and have been branded in my memory ever since that moment. He said, "In the cruise line business, one must be willing to serve. Service is an art. I have found that Americans, for the most part, don't want to serve. They want to *be* served."

That conversation is one that I will never forget. I was embarrassed and humbled to know that as a citizen of the United States, we were not only known as the wealthiest nation in the world, but we had a reputation for possibly being the most selfish. As I have recalled his words from time to time, I have prayed and asked God to help me remember the following important fact: The mark of a true Christian is not how good we look sitting in the pew in our church attire on Sunday.

Faith Lift

It is how well we serve others throughout the week.

Have you been too busy to help your neighbor at a time when he or she needed your help? When you heard of someone who was in trouble, did you find yourself muttering these words: "I just don't want to get involved"? As you read the story of the Good Samaritan, do you see yourself as the priest, the Levite or the Good Samaritan?

If you recognized yourself in the priest or the Levite, then you are in the right place to ask God's forgiveness for ignoring the needs of others and possibly behaving in a selfish manner. James 2:14–17 says:

> What good is it, my brothers, if a man claims to have faith but has no deeds? Can such faith save him? Suppose a brother or a sister is without clothes and daily food. If one of you says to him, "Go, I wish you well; keep warm and well fed," but does nothing about his physical needs, what good is it? In the same way, faith by itself, if it is not accompanied by action, is dead.

Do you know someone whose faith is sagging right now? Has the Lord brought someone to your mind whose spirit has been beaten down along life's road? It's guaranteed that someone within your sphere of influence could use a faith lift today. It's quite possible that the person who is in need will see Christ in your response to their plight.

Mother Teresa, known as the Angel of Mercy, demonstrated this compassionate lifestyle. She once said, "You and I, we are the Church, no? We have to share with our people. Suffering today is because people are hoarding, not giving, not sharing. Jesus made it very clear. Whatever you do to the least of my brethren, you do it to me. Give a glass of water, you give it to me. Receive a little child, you receive me. Clear?"[1]

I hope you can see things a little clearer. Remember this. It is good to be a Christian and know it. It is better to be a Christian and show it.

Therefore everyone who hears these words
of mine and puts them into practice is like a
wise man who built his house on the rock.

—MATTHEW 7:24

CHAPTER 5

Faith

Your Foundation

RECENTLY THE MASON family hosted our family reunion over the Fourth of July weekend. We all gathered at our rural country home. OK, it's a modular home. All right, it's a doublewide mobile house trailer. But it serves a great purpose when we want to get away for a weekend to fish and enjoy some much-needed solitude.

Now that our sons are grown, Charles and I have decided to move to the country permanently. Charles is a country boy who longs for the day when he can plant rows and rows of corn and watermelons and not be disappointed when he arrives to check on things on the Monday after a weekend road trip, only to find them nibbled up by the deer. I am not a country girl by any means. But years of airport visits, hotel stays and restaurant meals have left this city girl yearning for the simple life. We love our picturesque piece of rural property complete with rolling hills, pastures, woods and water. We have decided on the kind of house we want to build, and we have picked just the right spot high upon a hill with great views

The process of building a house is an arduous task. I am now learning the true meaning of the phrase "labor of love." The decisions and choices are endless. The challenges and deadlines are stressful. It's quite a tedious venture. But one day next winter when I am sitting in front of a crackling fire with a thick book and a cup of tea, I will have forgotten all the pains of decision making. The choices, challenges and deadlines will be nothing but a misty memory. For now, though, the fireplace is still on paper and the cup of tea and thick book are figments of my imagination.

When the family had gathered for the reunion, everyone was excited to see the progress we were making on the house, and we were ready to show them. We were in the very early stages of building. Huge mounds of dirt surrounded the site. Only the foundation had been laid. So only the concrete slabs and footings had been poured. If you really used your imagination, you could see the potential for a home.

We began shuttling family members up and down the hill in the golf cart to see our home's development. Four of the youngest members of our family, all boys around the age of ten, were anxious to see what was going on, too. So I loaded them up, and we headed for the top of the hill. We yahooed and hollered as we galloped over the bumps and jogs of virgin pasture. Reaching the height of the hill, I prepared to give my four passengers the tour of the site. But before I could begin my speech, the youngest of the four bucked his big brown eyes, pitched his voice high and yelled with ten-year-old delight, "Wow, look at that big ol' mountain of dirt! Let's go exploring. Geronimo!"

Like streaks of lightening, they took off, yipping and yelling to their heart's content. They hadn't given a moment's thought to the lecture that I was about to deliver. I was about to say, "But wait. Don't you want to hear about the square footage? I need to show you the room where I will write new songs. Look! Over here is where I plan to have coffee and morning devotions. And over here…" No way. See ya later, alligator.

Before I knew it, four rambunctious boys were off and running toward an enormous man-made mountain of red Georgia clay dirt. They had imaginary giants to slay and territories to claim. Of course, their mothers wanted to wring my neck for allowing that unforgiving red clay to ruin their white socks.

Over a period of many months, walls, floors, ceilings and windows would go in on top of that concrete foundation. At first glance, foundations are nothing pretty to look at. Gray concrete slabs, steel beams and lots of dirt don't say a whole lot to a woman like me who has already picked out the color scheme for the entire house. As I walked on that foundation, I began to get a better understanding of its function. I decided to slow down a bit and to look at the foundation a bit closer.

FOUNDATION BUILDING

Establishing the foundation is the first step in building a structure. The foundation will support the entire structure. Steel forms are placed below the ground level and then are filled with concrete to provide the needed strength for the walls. Everything else will stand on this foundation. The support system must be of sufficient size and strength to avoid excessive or uneven settlement, which could cause walls to crack, floors to be uneven or doors to hang improperly. Ultimately, the foundation will bear the weight of construction, plus the load of furnishings, appliances, pets and people.

The Bible says that there are two kinds of people. There are wise people who build their lives upon the firm foundation of God's principles from His Word, the Bible. Then there are foolish people who build their lives upon the world's principles and practices, which have no foundation at all.

Therefore everyone who hears these words of Mine,

and acts upon them, may be compared to a wise man, who built his house upon the rock. And the rain descended, and the floods came, and the winds blew, and burst against that house; and yet it did not fall, for it had been founded upon the rock. And everyone who hears these words of Mine, and does not act upon them, will be like a foolish man, who built his house upon the sand. And the rain descended, and the floods came, and the winds blew, and burst against that house; and it fell, and great was its fall.

—MATTHEW 7:24–27, NAS

Trusting in our own plans only leads down the slippery slope to despair and hopelessness.

Have you ever built a sandcastle? One of my favorite places to vacation is the beach. I like to sit alongside the ocean with a good book and watch the ships go by on a long, lazy, summer day. Although I haven't had much success, I like to build sand-castles. I have watched other vacationers spend hours building some of the most elaborate sandcastles I have ever seen.

Sandcastle builders know that there is an art to good construction. The sand has to be moist enough to stick together, but dry enough to maintain its shape. There's no end to the kinds of containers that can be used to create the shapes for the desired structure. I've seen castles with moats and two-story houses with balconies. After hours of work, I've seen those diligent builders pack up their pails and buckets and go home, leaving a beautiful sandcastle on the shore. It may be there for a while. But sand is only a temporary medium. It doesn't matter if you like your work of art or not. It won't be long before the ocean comes to claim it.

The fragile sandcastle just cannot endure the repeated pounding of the ocean's waves as the tide forces its way toward the shore. Or one of those surprising afternoon storms could rush in, bringing with it high winds and rain showers. As pretty as that sandcastle may be, it just can't take the pounding of the relentless rain and wind. Pretty soon there will not be even a trace of where that sandcastle used to stand.

Sadly enough, this is how some people live their lives. By experience, they learned that placing their hopes and dreams in people and things is a big mistake. I once met a young lady who searched for pleasure as a dancer in a strip club. In the beginning, she enjoyed the large tips and the attention she got from her male patrons. But the owner of the club soon expected more of her than a few dances. It didn't take very long before she was hooked on drugs and involved in a life of prostitution.

I heard the testimony of a young man who once lusted after money and power. He took pleasure in impressing his friends. Early on, he enjoyed the sense of success. But his drug dealing led to drug abuse. Soon, to support his habit, he became a habitual gambler. His cycle of abusive behavior led him to serve most of his adult life in prison.

Both of these precious people learned the hard way that trusting in their own plans only leads down the slippery slope to despair and hopelessness. In Proverbs 28:26, we read, "He who trusts in his own heart is a fool, but he who walks wisely will be delivered" (NAS). Psalm 20:7says, "Some trust in chariots and some in horses, but we trust in the name of the Lord our God."

King David, who prayed this prayer for victory during a time of trouble and great challenge, knew that those who are wise trust in the power of God more than in the power of people.

Great nations have been known to boast of their powerful weapons and skilled military troops. But David knew that his greatest strength was not in manpower, but in God's power.

Praise God, I know the end of both the stories I told above. The young lady ran away from her pimp at the counsel of a Christian lady who befriended her and took her into her home. Through care and discipleship, the young lady was led to Christ. She now operates a home that serves as a refuge for former prostitutes. The young man met Christ while serving time in prison. While incarcerated, he began to teach Bible studies. He is now out of prison and serving in the local church. He is married, with a family and is living drug free. Trusting in Christ makes all the difference.

Placing one's total confidence in anything but Christ is certain to bring disappointment sooner or later. Great numbers of people have placed their trust in the stock market, which is unpredictable at best. In seasons past, it has been possible to make a great deal of money. But recent events, such as September 11, 2001, have placed fear in the hearts of many. For reasons too numerous to mention, the nation's economy has suffered. Millions of dollars in investments have been lost, leaving Americans broke and fearful, wondering how this could have happened.

I have heard the personal stories of many who invested years of hard-earned income, faithfully putting a little aside for a rainy day, only to see it all go down the drain. The Word of God instructs us not to place our confidence in money. Proverbs 11:28 warns us, "Whoever trusts in his riches will fall, but the righteous will thrive like a green leaf."

For centuries, it has been the nature of man to seek the advice of psychics in order to search for a solid place to stand. Things are no different today. Since the birth of the informercial, we've seen the popularity of fortunetellers and psychics increase. With cunning finesse, psychics have convinced many gullible viewers that their futures could be predicted. In search of answers, people called in by the thousands with their problems.

But after much scrutiny, these psychics have turned out to be phonies. Many of these television programs have proven to be a waste of film and have gone by the way of bankruptcy court. Isn't it amazing, however, that their psychic hosts never saw it coming!

The Word of God tells us that this superstitious practice is evil. It may look and sound like truth, but truth and evil, like oil and water, do not mix. The Bible clearly tells us in Psalm 118:8, "It is better to take refuge in the Lord than to trust in man."

Whether your trust is in people or in things, both will disappoint and both will prove to be futile.

One's hope in this life, and in eternity, comes from trusting only in Christ.

Building a strong foundation is imperative for successful house building. It is also crucial for successful life building. The fool builds his life on shifting sand. But the wise man builds his life on the rock-solid, unchanging, foundational principles of truth—the transforming truths of God's Word, the Bible. The Bible says that the man who considers how he will build his house is wise. He plans ahead, and then he thinks things through.

> Suppose one of you wants to build a tower. Will he not first sit down and estimate the cost to see if he has enough money to complete it?
>
> —LUKE 14:28

The one who desires to live a life according to godly principles will look at where he is and determine where he needs to go and how he will get there. He will see himself as God sees him—lost, hopeless, dying and in need of a Savior. One's hope in this life, and in eternity, comes from trusting only in Christ.

As we continued the building of our house in the country, I began to see spiritual building principles come to life right before my eyes. At every stage of the building process, the county inspector would pay a visit to insure that the building was being constructed according to building codes. His determination would have to be made before the construction workers could move on to the next stage. If the foundation or any other part of the structure was not built according to his specification, it would not pass inspection.

Let me ask you, my friend, are there any parts of your life that are raising red flags under the watchful eye of your heavenly Inspector? If the foundation of your life stands strong and firm on the principles of the Bible, which you are applying to your life, your heart will be a place where Jesus will be right at home. It will be a place where He is pleased to dwell. There will be no leaky roof, no weak floors and no cracks in the windows. Only regular maintenance will be necessary.

The wise man not only hears the Word, but he heeds the Word. He puts it into practice. God has given us everything we need to live in this world and to prepare for the next.

His divine power has given us everything we need for
life and godliness through our knowledge of him who
called us by his own glory and goodness.

—2 PETER 1:3

The Word of God ought to have first place in your life.
Everything you do—all of your thoughts and actions—should
be filtered through the sieve of truth. Billy Graham's daughter
Gigi Graham Tchividjian said, "Weave the unveiling fabric of
God's Word through your heart and mind. It will hold strong,
even if the rest of life unravels."[1]

I have a vivid memory of riding around town in our car as
a young girl with my father as he listened to Bible study teacher
Dr. J. Vernon McGee. Dr. McGee's program would always
begin with the song "How Firm a Foundation." Motown music
lover that I was, in my opinion, the hymn was old, stale and
meaningless to me. Today, my father and Dr. McGee have
graduated to glory. The fruit of their ministries remain along
with this timeless, old hymn.

How firm a foundation, ye saints of the Lord,
Is laid for your faith in His excellent Word!
What more can He say than to you He hath said,
To you who for refuge to Jesus have fled?

"Fear not, I am with thee; O be not dismayed,
For I am thy God, and will still give thee aid;
I'll strengthen thee, help thee, and cause thee to stand,
Upheld by My righteous, omnipotent hand.

"When through fiery trials thy pathway shall lie,
My grace, all sufficient, shall be thy supply:
The flame shall not hurt thee; I only design
Thy dross to consume, and thy gold to refine.

"The soul that on Jesus hath leaned for repose

I will not, I will not desert to his foes;
That soul, though all hell should endeavor to shake,
I'll never, no, never, no, never forsake!"[2]

Do you desire to be a temple, a place of worship where Jesus is pleased to dwell? Don't worry about good-looking stained-glass windows or manicured landscapes. Start with a solid foundation. All those other things will take care of themselves.

For God hath not given us the spirit of fear; but of power, and of love, and of a sound mind.

—2 TIMOTHY 1:7, KJV

CHAPTER 6

Faith

Your Fears

ON TUESDAY, SEPTEMBER 11, 2001, our world was rocked. Our entire nation was horrified as we witnessed the horrible events of the terrorist attacks on the World Trade Center, the Pentagon and on those who perished aboard the flight in Pennsylvania. Those events ricocheted across the nation, sending our country into a state of emergency. The very core of our modern society was challenged as never before, and we are still reeling from the deadly blows.

The threat of terror still lurks around every corner. The cleanup process has ended at Ground Zero where the Twin Towers of the World Trade Center once stood. But painful memories remain. The word *terror* has become a frequently used word in our vocabulary. Americans are still apprehensive to go back to what was a normal routine. Nothing is the way it used to be.

Journalists are now calling the era in which we live *The New Normal.* More Americans stayed home for Thanksgiving and Christmas 2001 than ever before. Letters containing deadly anthrax took precious lives and threatened the safety of our country's mail system. Our country's officials and our business leaders tell us to resume our lives as normal. They encourage us to travel as usual and to spend our money. They are confident that if we get out into the shopping malls and airports it will boost America's sagging economy. But one major factor keeps us close to home, clinching tightly to our wallets. That factor is fear.

I didn't know anyone personally who perished in the attacks of September 11. But just like every American, my life has definitely been affected. On the day of the attacks, my family and friends were all in a state of shock as we gathered around the television to watch the unbelievable events of that day. Several of our neighbors gathered at our home to reach out to each other. Our family felt uncomfortable and disjointed because my husband was stranded out on the West Coast while visiting family.

It just so happened that my concert schedule allowed me to be singing around the state of Georgia for the following three weeks. I was relieved that I didn't have to get on a plane. However, as the first week of October approached, I knew I would have to be in Michigan. I had made up in my mind that I was going to drive. I felt good about that decision. Our son had agreed to help me make the twelve-hour trip up north and back.

Then the airline of which I am a frequent flier member began offering frequent flier awards for free travel for almost half the points. I was faced with a dilemma: Should I drive or fly? I rationalized all the pros and cons in my head. If I drove the twelve hours up and back, I would be dog-tired upon my arrival, and I would be spending most of the weekend on the road. But I would feel as if I had more control over my own safety.

If I flew, I would get there a whole lot faster, but I felt that safety would be an issue. I had to face it—I was afraid to fly. At that point, I realized I had a problem. I had allowed myself to be consumed with uncontrollable fear. The thought of getting on an airplane sent me into bouts of panic. I'd catch myself playing out scenarios in my mind. Then I'd pray about the situation, and I'd feel better for the moment. Like a yo-yo on a string, I would go back and forth between decisions.

> *I believed that His perfect love for me, my love for Him and the work that I had to do that weekend would cast out all my fear—and it did.*

I finally concluded that, realistically, the deal the airline had made was just too good to pass up. It was two free tickets and an hour-and-forty-five-minute flight, compared to a twelve-hour drive and feeling like a whipped puppy upon our arrival. There was no comparison. The decision was made. We would fly to Michigan. The days prior to that flight kept me in a constant inner battle between my flesh and my spirit. One moment I was certain that everything would be fine. The next, I wondered if that plane would be the last plane ride I'd ever take.

The first weekend in October came. That Friday morning I got up and committed my day to the Lord and headed for the airport. As I went through the security process, I realized that air travel as I'd known it before September 11 was a thing of the past. I boarded the airplane that day, and, as I often do, I grabbed the Bible that I kept in the outside pocket of my carry-on bag. I began to pray even while people were still boarding the plane. I asked God to keep us and deliver us all to Detroit safely. I placed my carry-on into the overhead compartment and took my seat. I buckled my seat belt and opened my Bible, only to discover it was not the version of the study Bible that I usually carry with me. On the last trip I must have taken out my study Bible and replaced it with a copy of *The Message*. I turned to Psalm 91 and began to read.

> You who sit down in the High God's presence,
>   spend the night in Shaddai's shadow,
> Say this; "GOD, you're my refuge.
>   I trust in you and I'm safe!"
> That's right—he rescues you from hidden traps,
>   shields you from deadly hazards.
> His huge outstretched arms protect you—
>   under them you're perfectly safe;
>   his arms fend off all harm.
> Fear nothing—not wild wolves in the night,
>   not flying arrows in the day,
> Not disease that prowls through the darkness,
>   not disaster that erupts at high noon.
> Even though others succumb all around,
>   drop like flies right and left,
>   no harm will even graze you.
> You'll stand untouched, watch it all from a distance,
>   watch the wicked turn into corpses.
> Yes, because GOD's your refuge,
>   the High God your very home,
> Evil can't get close to you,
>   harm can't get through the door.
> He ordered his angels
>   to guard you wherever you go.
> If you stumble, they'll catch you;

their job is to keep you from falling.
You'll walk unharmed among lions and snakes
   and kick young lions and serpents from the path.

"If you'll hold on to me for dear life," says GOD,
   "I'll get you out of any trouble.
I'll give you the best of care
   if you'll only get to know and trust me.
Call me and I'll answer, be at your side in bad times;
   I'll rescue you, then throw you a party.
I'll give you a long life,
   give you a long drink of salvation!"

—PSALM 91, THE MESSAGE

Having that Bible in my luggage for that flight was no mistake. That is exactly what I needed to hear at that exact moment. I consider Psalm 91:1 to be the verse I remember when I am facing my own state of emergency. God had hand-picked a message that He wanted me to hear and delivered it right to my seat. As I buckled my seat belt and felt it snugly holding me in, I sensed the security of His sweet presence around me and in me, accompanied by his unfailing love for me. I believed that His perfect love for me, my love for Him and the work that I had to do that weekend would cast out all my fear—and it did. I closed my Bible, whispered a prayer of thanks to God, leaned back in my seat and took a nap.

DON'T TAKE YOUR EYES OFF JESUS

When the apostle Peter stepped out of the boat at the Sea of Galilee in Matthew 14:25–32, his heart responded with faith. At that moment, his faith in Jesus was so strong that, at Jesus' command, Peter began to walk on the water. He even asked the Lord to call for him. Peter stepped out of the boat and began to walk toward his Friend and Savior. For one moment he defied the laws of nature. At the next, reality and reason set in. He felt the stormy winds whirling around his body. He saw the rolling ocean waves dashing under his feet.

That's when Peter took his eyes off Jesus and placed them on his unbelievable situation. Immediately, he began to sink into the deep, dark, stormy sea. I was a lot like that. Peter and I are very much alike. In our hearts, we knew that God is a God of the impossible. But the weight of the moment tempted us to take our eyes off Jesus and to put them on our circumstances. That is when doubt overwhelmed us and began to take us under. We found ourselves drowning in the depths of despair. But praise God, just when we were going under, we cried out for help, and Jesus reached out and caught us.

If you gave it some thought, you would probably admit that you've come face to face with the spirit of fear at one time or another. The possibility is great that you've tasted the bitterness of fear somewhere along the way. Maybe since September 11 you too have felt a fear so gripping that it paralyzed you. Maybe it colored your decisions. Maybe it kept you from boarding an airplane. Maybe you thought twice before getting on an elevator in a high-rise building. Maybe fear kept you from driving on the expressway. Maybe you had a feeling of panic as you wondered about a piece of mail that had been delivered to your home or office.

It could be that fear caused you to grip your purse a little tighter in the shopping mall. Letting your small children play outside unsupervised is out of the question now. Do you sleep with the lights on? It could be that you are more suspicious of your neighbors' activities than ever before.

Fear—it will hold you as a prisoner in its suffocating grip until you are afraid to move. That is when you must remind yourself that the spirit of fear is not from God. God has given you weapons to use for your defense—the Word of God, prayer and praise. They are the most powerful weapons you have at your disposal. They will release the very presence of God into your situation. Wherever the presence of God is, the enemy has to flee!

LESSONS ABOUT FEAR

I learned a great deal in that season when I came face to face with the spirit of fear. I knew I could find the answers to my challenges in the Bible. I began to study one of my favorite stories. Once again, it bolstered my faith. The story is found in 2 Chronicles 20:1–30. This remarkable story is a picture of God's people when they were most vulnerable. But it is also a demonstration of God's mighty power on display. In spite of the odds, in spite of what it may look like, almighty God is for you. As Romans 8:31 says, "If God is for us, who can be against us?"

> *Wherever the presence of God is, the enemy has to flee!*

1. God is on my side.

The first thing I learned is this: *There is a God, and He is on my side. I must work with Him.* I encourage you to make that confession aloud:

> There is a God, and He is on my side. I must work with Him.

Jehoshaphat, king over Judah, had received word that three

vast armies—the Moabites, the Ammonites and the Meunites—were coming to annihilate him and his people. Look at Jehoshaphat's response:

> Alarmed, Jehoshaphat resolved to inquire of the LORD, and he proclaimed a fast for all Judah. The people of Judah came together to seek help from the LORD; indeed, they came from every town in Judah to seek him.
>
> —2 CHRONICLES 20:3–4

Look at what Jehoshaphat *did not do. He did not panic*, although he was alarmed. *He did not take matters into his own hands.* His back was against the wall. The odds were against him. He knew that his people were outnumbered. Instead, he immediately went to God for help. *He did not forget God's promises.* He allowed the promises of God to go to work for Him. Calling the entire nation to a time of prayer and fasting, Jehoshaphat believed that they would win this battle with divine intervention. Making a choice decision, he decided to do things God's way. When he prayed, he prayed according to God's promises, relying upon the faithfulness of God.

You have a choice. You can choose the blessings, or you can choose the curses. A dear friend once encouraged me with these words, "You can look out of one window of your house and see the sun shining. You can look out of another window and see the clouds. You decide which window you're going to look out." Take this to heart, my friend. Be like Jehoshaphat. Regardless of the outcome, God's people choose to do things God's way.

2. I must resist the enemy.

Second, I learned this: *There is an enemy, and he is against me. I must resist him.* The devil has one mission. That mission is to kill you, to steal from you and to destroy you. He will make it his business to torment you and to cause you nothing but pain and misery. On the weekend after the terrorist attack in September, I attended a conference where I was the guest singer. It was only ninety miles from my house, so I was relieved to be driving to the conference center. That Saturday evening after the meeting, all the speakers gathered in one room to pray. I had expressed my concern about this fear of flying to my colleagues. One of my speaker friends offered some insight. The moment the words came out of her mouth, I realized they were words from God. She said, "Babbie, I believe the enemy has targeted you." That's all she had to say. That rang like an alarm in my spirit, and I sat up straight and thought about it. She was right.

I processed her words in my mind: *Targeted me? Those words sound like fighting words! Well, I don't think so.* I pictured myself with a bull's-eye on my back. *I'm not going to be a target for anybody,* I thought. *I refuse to be a sitting duck for the enemy. It's hard to hit a moving target. So, I'd better be up and about my Father's business.*

> *Whenever God comes on the scene, fear, with its torment, has to go.*

That's all it took. My eyes were opened, and I realized that this was a plot the enemy was trying to use to destroy me. This was no fear of flying. This was warfare! It was not the emotion of fear that I was facing; it was the spirit of fear. Once I grasped hold of that revelation, I was determined not to be a helpless victim. I remembered the passage from 2 Chronicles 20:15:

> Listen, King Jehoshaphat and all who love in Judah
> and Jerusalem! This is what the LORD says to you: "Do
> not be afraid or discouraged because of this vast army.
> For the battle is not yours, but God's."

Right then and there, I asked God to fight this battle for me.
Praise God, He has.

Someone has said that the words "fear not" are mentioned
366 times in the Bible. That would be one mention for each
day, including a leap year. Well, I don't know if that's true or
not. But I have started to keep a record of them. In my study of
those words, I have discovered one thing. Wherever the words
"fear not" appear in the Scriptures, good news always follows
close behind. Check it out and see for yourself. Whenever God
comes on the scene, fear, with its torment, has to go. Good
news and the hope of things to come are positioned right there
with Him.

3. God is in control.

Last of all remember this: *There is a God, and He is in control.
I must yield to Him.* Jesus is Lord over fear. And Jesus is Lord
over your enemy, the devil. Philippians 2:10 proclaims that
every knee will bow to the authority of the name of Jesus. That
means Satan will bow, too! When faced with fear, remind yourself of the fact that God is in control of your situation. Do not
be moved by what you feel. This is the time to stand on what
you know to be truth. Your ammunition is the Word of God.

The level of your faith is directly related to how much of the
Word of God you actually have hidden in your heart. The more
the Word occupies your heart, the less room there is for fear to
reside there. The devil will come against you to cause you to
doubt God and what He has said. This is not the time for passive faith. This is the time for the kind of faith that puts up a

fight. God is not looking for wimps, but believers with back-bone. He is enlisting those who will do mighty exploits for Him.

When you are in the middle of a test and the pressure is on, it is your responsibility to be prepared already with the knowl-edge that will allow you to pass the test. A decision to trust God must already be made. You must already have the weapon of the Word inside you. Even during an open-book test, you must still know where to look.

Give God control of it all. Don't try to hold on to the little things that you think you can control. Leave each and every detail up to God. If your heart is giving way to fear, don't just run from it. Instead, run to the Lord with your burden of fear. He will take it and replace it with His peace. Instead of focus-ing on your fear, concentrate on how much God loves you and how perfectly He cares for you. When you are tempted to fear, look for the way of escape. God has provided a way out.

> There is no fear in love. But perfect love drives out fear.
>
> —1 JOHN 4:18

The events of September 11 may have rocked our nation and our world. But God was not the least bit moved. Our nation may be at war, and our economy may be faltering. In spite of our own personal challenges and changes, God has not changed. He remains the same. He remains faithful and trust-worthy. He knows our end from our beginning, and as long as our trust remains in Him, and only in Him, our foundation and our faith will be the force that sustains us as a nation, as a church and as believers.

Proverbs 18:10 says, "The name of the Lord is a strong tower; the righteous run to it and are safe." What mental picture do you get when you think of a tower? In this post-September-11 world, it's easy to picture a tower filled with disaster. Let the

Lord use this powerful passage to change the mental pictures that you see. Think of the Lord's name as being a place where you are safe from disaster, disease, despair, depression and any other potentially harmful situation.

The next time fear tries to come upon you, picture yourself like a well-trained baseball player who makes the most of his opportunity to steal from first to second base with lightning speed. With help from a very wise Coach, you will find yourself resting on the base safe and sound and ready at any moment to head for home. Picture yourself finding a hiding place in the Lord where nothing and no one can harm you or remove you. When you think of the words, *The righteous run to it and are safe,* picture an umpire's signal, safe.

Giants have a history of coming out on the losing end when the giant slayer has God on his side.

Don't let Satan use fear to discourage you and to rob you of your spiritual stamina. Don't allow him to put fear upon you. The enemy will use fear to distract you and to try to get you to take your eyes off Jesus. Don't let him do it. He'll use fear to distort the truths of God's Word that you already know to be true. Don't give him any room. The devil will use fear to tempt you to disobey God's voice. Don't listen.

Instead, take a look at God's perfect track record. Remind yourself of what He has done for you in the past and what He promises to do for you in the future. Do you really believe that the Word of God is true? Do you know other circumstances where God has been faithful? If the answer is yes, then begin to practice the presence of God. Remember that He is God, and He has every detail of your life under His control. Fear may appear like a stalking giant who is seconds away from consuming you. Well, giants have a history of coming out on the losing end when the giant slayer has God on his side. That giant was not too big to hit. That giant was too big to miss. Your giant may be big, but he's no match for a great big God.

Noted author Catherine Marshall encourages us to run to God with our fears by saying this:

> If your every human plan and calculation has miscarried—if, one by one human props have been knocked out, take heart. God is trying to get a message through to you, and the message is: "Stop depending on inadequate human resources. Let me handle the matter."

If you are consumed with fear by day, and your fears are even keeping you up at night, remember that God never sleeps or slumbers. Put your fears to rest. Your heavenly Father will be up all night, so you might as well get some sleep.

For I am persuaded, that neither death, nor life, nor angels, nor principalities, nor powers, nor things present, nor things to come, nor height, nor depth, nor any other creature, shall be able to separate us from the love of God, which is in Christ Jesus our Lord.

—ROMANS 8:38–39, KJV

CHAPTER 7

Faith

Your Failures

I ONCE HEARD A story about a little boy who was having difficulty lifting a heavy stone. His father came along just then. Noting the boy's failure, he asked, "Are you using all your strength?"

"Yes, I am," the little boy said impatiently.

"No, you are not," the father answered. "I am right here just waiting, and you haven't asked me to help you."

That little story reminds me that we can do nothing that is effective on our own. We need the help of God, *Jehovah Jireh, the One who provides.* Recently, I met a remarkable woman whose relentless faith gave her the strength to climb up the mountain of despair and raise high the flag of hope.

The moment that Ruth Jones walked up the steps of the old dilapidated elementary school building, she felt her heart fill up with hopelessness. She was aware of her assignment—to reopen the school as its new principal. Not a single child from this school had gone on to college in over ten years, and 75 percent of the students did not graduate from high school. The institution's reputation had preceded itself. In the past, students who had walked the halls actually had stalked the halls. Fighting was nonstop, and teachers ruled the students through intimidation and humiliation. As she walked through the front doors and down the vacant hallways, Ruth Jones felt a huge wave of apprehension. She saw this fierce foe, a dark, decaying inner-city school standing like a mountain before her. But deep in her spirit she knew this was her destiny. Ruth Jones, a woman of faith, was on a mission from God and was prepared to call those things that are not as though they were.

One day in 1993, it had been announced in Mrs. Jones's city's newspaper that the school would be closing. That evening she had received a phone call from the assistant superintendent of the school district. The caller told Mrs. Jones that there would be a meeting that evening on the playground to save the school. "We'd like you to think about heading up this project," the woman said.

Mrs. Jones was shocked. She made it clear that she had no administrative experience, neither did she have a master's degree. Mrs. Jones made it perfectly clear that she loved teaching and had no desire to be a principal. The assistant superintendent was aware of all that. In fact, Mrs. Jones was already being considered for the position. Her file was already at the office on the desk of the superintendent of schools.

Ruth Jones loved her job as a seventh- and eighth-grade social studies and language arts teacher. As a black woman teaching blacks and minorities in the inner city, she believed that the foundation for successful teaching was based on love. For years, she had practiced the principles of love and learning in her classroom. She knew this philosophy worked. Her students had won awards at the state and national levels. Many of them excelled ahead of suburban white students.

She felt God impressing her to interview for the job. But she didn't want the job, and she resisted. The more she resisted, the more God persisted.

She decided that at her interview she would tell the interview committee of this public school district about the Lord and how He had changed her life. She would tell them that she didn't want the job, but she knew she was supposed to take it. She would tell them how God was at the center of her educational philosophy. After hearing her story, if they still wanted this rock-solid Christian woman to be the principal of this public school, then she would know it was God's doing.

During the interview, she explained, "God is bringing me here to this school because He wants to heal the hearts of these children and give them a chance at life." Mrs. Jones was willing to lay her beliefs and even her job on the line. At the end of the interview, the entire room was in tears. There were others who wanted the job and were qualified to handle its challenges. But by unanimous decision, the Grand Rapids Board of Education named Ruth Jones the new principal of Henry Paideia Academy.

Today, nine years later, laughter fills the halls and artwork graces the walls of the school, which houses grades kindergarten through seven. About the award-winning school, Mrs. Jones says, "It's a miracle. God is doing it, and I'm right in the middle of it all." Like a loving mother, she speaks words of faith into the lives of her students. Showering them with praise, she calls the affirming words that she speaks *terms of endearment*. Each day she touches their lives with words she knows some may rarely hear at home. Words like, "Great job, Sweetheart." "I knew you could do it, Precious." "I am depending on you, Honey." "You are a leader. You must behave like one."

She instructs the school's teachers to do the same. She says that instead of beating a child down with words, we should "praise them up." She also showers them with love. During lunch, on a daily basis, the children are given the gift of quiet time when every student is allowed to reflect upon his or her dreams, aspirations and blessings or read a favorite book. Following the quiet time, as the children pass by on their way back to class, she hugs a neck, pinches a cheek or pats a back. She and God are in covenant. She believes the anointing destroys the enemy's strongholds, and as she touches each child, she prays for God to destroy depression, dullness, anger and mental deficiencies. Children who come into the school hardhearted and callous are soon tenderized by love.

"Faith is everything to me," Ruth Jones responds. "If I didn't know God, I would not have touched the school. I knew I was going to be in for some hard work. Demons were entrenched in the very fabric of the school. This was enemy territory. But, 'It's not by might, nor by power, but by My Spirit, says the Lord.' I believe in the power of God. Only God can clean up messes and turn them into blessings."

The children who have been blessed to be under such dedicated administration have gone on to become a blessing to others. Some students have gone on to various colleges and are members of the Honor Society and other prestigious organizations.

"Only God can clean up messes and turn them into blessings."

Ruth Jones believes that love does cover a multitude of sins. "If you sow nothing, you reap nothing. If you sow love, you reap love." Love is at the basis of everything she does. The school has even adopted, as its theme, a song I was privileged to write called, "Love Is the More Excellent Way." At each assembly or school function, the student body, faculty and parents can be heard singing in the school gym:

> Love is patient
> Love is kind
> Love is humble
> All of the time
> Not easily angered
> Enduring the test
> So never forget
> Love is the more
> Excellent way.[1]

A truly inspirational woman, Ruth Jones is a master at teaching students to overcome their failures by sowing seeds of success and greatness. She believes that in each child God has deposited a gift to offer the world, whether the child comes from the suburbs or the inner city. She has said "Wouldn't it be just like God to put the cure for cancer in the minds of one of the poor inner-city kids? And because we don't invest in these children, we'll never get the cure." Wouldn't it be something if when we get to heaven we'll ask God why we didn't get a cure for cancer, and God may say, "The answer was in one of the inner-city kids. But you didn't sow there."

Henry Elementary at one time had the highest number of student suspensions. Now the renamed Henry Paideia Academy has a waiting list for families who want their children to experience this school of higher learning. Visitors come from many states to tour and observe this model school. Always a feature in the news for its accolades, Ruth Jones lives out the true meaning of the school's name. *Paideia* is Greek for "the upbringing of a child." Ruth Jones is determined to do just that by staying on the walk of faith, by putting one foot in front of the other and never looking back.

Just as those children are blessed to be under the leadership and tutelage of such an able administrator, every one of us is under the watchful eye of our heavenly Father who "is able to do exceeding abundantly above all that we ask or think, according to the power that worketh in us" (Eph. 3:20, KJV). *According to the power that is at work within us…* God's power is not limited to a certain group of people. But He chooses and uses whomever He desires. People with past failures are prime candidates. Maybe your failures have beaten you down to size. If so, then praise God. While it is possible to be too big for God to use you, you are never too small for God to use you.

Whatever your history, the Lord wants to use you to accomplish His will and His work.

YOUR HISTORY IS NOT A FACTOR

In Matthew 1:1–17 we find the lineage of Jesus Christ. Down through two thousand years, forty-two generations and across the span of forty-six lives, we find some very interesting people in the family tree. A plethora of personalities, backgrounds and experiences—some like Abraham, Isaac, Ruth and David— were heroes and "she-roes" of the faith. Some we would consider spiritual giants, like Abraham, Isaac and Jacob. Others were known to have questionable character, like Rahab and Tamar who were known to be prostitutes. Others were quite average like Nahshon and Akim. Still other descendants were evil like Manasseh, who worshiped idol gods and sacrificed his children to them. In the lineage of Jesus there are those whose lives are considered success stories. Then there are those who would be labeled failures.

What's your story? What are the highlights of your experience, good, bad or indifferent? Have you been raised in church and had a history of walking with the Lord most of your life? Do you feel rather average and that you kind of fade into anonymity? Maybe you have had a brush or two with the law and you come with a rap sheet. Whatever your history, the Lord wants to use you to accomplish His will and His work. Regardless of past failures, no matter what others may have said about you, what God says about you is really what matters.

Ruth Jones said, "Only God can clean up messes and turn them into blessings. He certainly took all the messes in my life, and through the ministry I'm involved in at Henry, He has turned my life into a blessing." That goes for the messes in your life as well. Somehow, God can use your failures as a launching pad for your victories. Some way, somewhere down the line you will see that "all things work together for good to those who love God, to those who are the called according to His purpose" (Rom. 8:28, NKJV). Don't forget. It's not over until God has the last word.

IT'S NOT OVER UNTIL GOD HAS THE LAST WORD

Once I had the privilege to interview speaker and author Cathy Phillips on *Babbie's House*, my TV talk show. When she was growing up, her family lived on a farm in the middle Georgia town of Newnan. On the farm, they raised hogs, cows, chicken and other farm animals. It was a challenge to feed a family and the animals, too. Oftentimes they did not have enough slop to feed their hogs. So Cathy's father made arrangements with a really nice local family-owned restaurant in the town to pick up the leftover food scraps from the plates of their customers. Twice during the week and once on Sunday, Cathy's father would drive her and her siblings over to the restaurant in the family's work truck to collect the pig slop in two 55-gallon drums. Sunday was the biggest day. The restaurant was known far and wide for its Sunday buffet. That was the ultimate feast for the restaurant's patrons. On Sunday after church, the Methodists and the Baptists were in a race to see who could get there first.

Because the busboys would have to clean the tables in a hurry to accommodate the rush of customers, silverware would often accidentally end up in the food scraps that got tossed out. Inevitably, the restaurant's good silverware would end up in the pig slop. One day after the pigs had eaten the slop, Cathy saw something shiny glistening in the sun. Much to her surprise, forks, spoons and knives lay at the bottom of the pig's trough. After a good washing and sterilizing, Cathy's mother tried to return the silverware to the restaurant. But the manager, a little put off by the idea, refused her offer and told her she could keep the pieces. Soon Cathy's mother had collected an entire silver service for eight, including all the serving pieces.

God does the very same thing with our lives. He finds us at the bottom of the pig slop of life, lifts us up out of our messy situations, cleans us up until we are bright and shiny and finds a place where we can be used. You are a success when you realize that at the end of your failure is the beginning of your victory. So don't forget. It's not over until God has the last word.

Do you have the faith to believe that God can take your worst mistakes and turn them around and use them for your good? I hope so. That is just what the Bible says God will do, if you allow Him.

GOD'S AMAZING GRACE

In Habakkuk 1:5, God told the people of Jerusalem that He would do some amazing things through them. Read aloud what the Word of God says:

> Look at the nations and watch—and be utterly amazed. For I am going to do something in your days that you would not believe, even if you were told.

As I read the Bible, I have gotten in the practice of putting my name in the place of the nouns and pronouns as they refer to the people of God. Then I claim that promise as if it were written to me personally. You should try that. It will give you a boost, a faith-filled mind-set. The Bible was written to you and me *personally*. Every promise in the Book, from cover to cover, belongs to us *personally*.

When it comes to God turning messes into blessings, the story of a great hymn writer comes to mind. John Newton, a white Englishman, left home and school at the age of eleven to begin life as a rough, depraved seaman. Eventually he became involved in the despicably evil occupation of buying and selling slaves, capturing them from their native land of West Africa and selling them around the world. As a slave trader, he preyed on the lives of black Africans, mercilessly tearing them away from their families and separating them from their homeland. This wicked man was even known to have victimized countless women slaves while aboard the slave ship.

Years later, while at sea, John Newton was caught in a fierce storm. Stunned with fear and afraid of a shipwreck, he cried out to God for help. God rescued him. This incident led him to a dramatic conversion experience that would change John Newton's life forever. God saved this man, cleansed him of a dreadful past, restored him to his rightful mind and gave him a clean heart and a brand-new start. Soon he began sensing that God was calling him to study for the ministry. This man, who once called himself a "wretch," became an ordained minister of the Anglican Church in a little village of Olney, England. Greatly influenced by John and Charles Wesley, his friends and fellow colleagues in the ministry and fellow songwriters, Newton began to use simple hymns in his services rather than just using the Psalms.

Wanting to express his own testimony in the form of a song, one morning John Newton introduced from the pulpit of his church a new song that God had blessed him to compose. He wanted this song to tell what God had done for him. That song was the great hymn "Amazing Grace."

> Amazing grace! how sweet the sound,
> That saved a wretch like me!
> I once was lost, but now am found,
> Was blind, but now I see.[2]

The unique thing about this hymn is that the melody is written on the pentatonic scale. The tune is centered around the five black notes on the keyboard of the piano. The Negro spirituals that were brought to America by African slaves were written and sung on the pentatonic or five-note scale. "Amazing Grace," whose powerful lyrics were written by a white man from England, is an African melody line.

Isn't that just like God to use a melody that John Newton certainly heard coming from the belly of his own slave ship? Isn't it like God to use a life marred by sin to birth something so simple, yet so profound? This melody was moaned by African men and women, homesick for a land they would never see again and terrified of what lay ahead. As those melodies, songs of grief and angst, swelled up out of the slave hold below, the Holy Spirit lay hold of John Newton's heart and planted a seed that would reap a song that would be sung around the world. Only God could use a life that was once filled with disgrace, and one who thought nothing of disgracing others, to birth one of the most beautiful hymns that the world has ever sung.

> 'Twas grace that taught my heart to fear,
> And grace my fears relieved;
> How precious did that grace appear
> The hour I first believed.

The apostle Paul tells us, "Where sin abounded, grace did much more abound" (Rom. 5:20, KJV). *Grace.* No matter how deep into sin you may have fallen, grace will go deeper still. If God can change a man whose lustful heart was filled with hatred and wrath, a man the likes of John Newton, surely God is able to change your heart and shout a proclamation of grace at the obstacles in your life and bring them crashing down. Maybe you have disgraced yourself and others by committing some unforgivable act. Did you make a mistake by prejudging someone before you knew all the facts? Have you condemned yourself or someone else, and your heart is cluttered with anger and resentment, even hatred?

You may have a reputation that has preceded you, and what others think and say about you is true. But God is able to do an "about faith" in your life, to turn things around for you. God is able to replace your disgrace, anger, resentment, bitterness, disappointment, disillusionment, disgust and even hatred with joy unspeakable and full of glory. Give all the messes you have created with your life to Jesus. He can handle it. He wants you to know today that there is nothing you could ever do that could keep Him from loving you. Romans 8:38–39 fills my heart with boundless hope and raises my faith to a new level:

> For I am persuaded, that neither death, nor life, nor

angels, nor principalities, nor powers, nor things present, nor things to come, nor height, nor depth, nor any
other creature, shall be able to separate us from the
love of God, which is in Christ Jesus our Lord.

—KJV

I believe that covers everything. Do you believe it, too?

You can see that I am not trying to please you by sweet talk and flattery; no, I am trying to please God. If I were still trying to please men I could not be Christ's servant.

—GALATIANS 1:10, TLB

CHAPTER 8

Faith

Your Frustrations

Have you ever been to the circus and seen the act that features the man who spins plates? It's amazing. He begins his act by spinning one plate at the end of a long pole. Then he puts the spin on the second plate, then a third. As plates begin to wobble, he runs back and forth, quickly rotating each plate. Before you know it, this plate spinner has seven, eight, nine, even ten plates all on the end of their slender poles, spinning at the same time. You gasp for breath as one plate begins to teeter, then another. Periodically he'll have to dash like a maniac to keep the plates from crashing to the floor. The audience loves it. One by one he takes each spinning plate off its pencil-like axis, holds each one safely in his arms and finally takes his bow.

Don't you wish that your plate-spinning scenarios were that simple? At the end of each day you would collect all the details of your life, put them away until tomorrow and kindly take a bow.

But that would be fantasy. This life we live is reality. If your life is anything like mine, you often find yourself getting one project off the ground, and then another and yet another. You seem to have your act together, but only for a moment. All it takes is one distraction to break your rhythm. Then the next thing you know, all of your plates are crashing down around you. Right now you may be burning the candle at both ends, running around like the proverbial chicken with its head cut off, in an effort to keep everything together.

Does a typical day in your life sound a little like this? You rise and shine at an hour you'd prefer to see only once a day in the P.M., get dressed, get the kids up, dressed, fed and off to school, then you hurry off to work. You put in a hard day on the job. You rush home to get the kids to baseball practice and piano lessons, then you rush back home, prepare dinner, help the kids with homework and get them off to bed. Then you do the dishes, do a load of laundry, read a few e-mails, prepare for tomorrow, shower and fall into bed. You sleep fast, then get up and do it all over again.

And as though that weren't enough, you have to add some unexpected inconveniences—a flat tire, a speeding ticket, a bounced check, a pink slip from your husband's job, a phone call from a teacher, a fender bender, a traffic jam, a long line at the grocery store, a delayed flight, a call from a bill collector or too much month and not enough money. Stop! "Calgon, take me away!"

No matter how big my problem is, God is bigger.

I can identify with you if you want to run away from it all. But before you run to your bathroom and lock the door behind you for some peace and quiet, let me tell you that you are not alone. Everyone has experienced that helpless feeling of frustration—that feeling you get when everything is in a mess and out of your control.

There is hope for you, because Jesus holds the keys that will release you from your prison of disturbance. The following story will lift your spirit. The story begins with a family friend who is very dear to the Mason family. In his own words, I'll let him tell his story.

> I had just relocated from Laurel, Mississippi, to Atlanta, Georgia. That's sort of like stepping out of a little pond into a big ocean. I quickly found myself in the middle of the deep end. My life's situation was over my head, and I was drowning in chaos. I was doing my best to get acclimated to a new job and helping my sons, eight and ten years old, adjust to a new school. If that was not enough shock for one's social system, add to that the fact that I was recently divorced and adjusting to single parenting.
>
> On top of all that, one of my boys was rollerblading at an apartment complex and skated down a steep slope and wandered into the flow of traffic. He was hit by an oncoming automobile and dragged a substantial distance! He was hospitalized with a broken leg, but he had no head injuries. Thank God for a miraculous outcome. However, he had a colostomy that I had to maintain and manage for several weeks.
>
> But the time had come when we were finally together and living in Marietta, Georgia. It was Tuesday morning in the fall of the year, and school was in full swing. It was a challenge getting used to added responsibility and a new schedule. I often found myself racing to get the boys up on time, dressed, fed and off to school. One day, in an effort to get everybody where they needed to be, and get them there on time, we raced to the car and off toward the school.

In the midst of my racing, I looked in my rear view mirror to find someone racing after me! You guessed it right. It was the police. He pulled me over. I gave him my license and sat there waiting. He came back to my car and proceeded to tell me that my driver's license had been previously revoked because I had neglected to renew my automobile insurance. I was totally in shock because I thought my license and my car insurance were current.

At that point, everything really began to fall apart. Now mind you, I don't have any family in Marietta, and I'd only been in Georgia for a few months. I didn't know very many people except the people I worked with. I hardly knew any people in my neighborhood. However, Charles and Babbie Mason lived around the corner from me, although at that time I did not know them well. But I'm sure they would have helped me if I had only had their phone number.

So there I was. I was stopped on the side of the road by a threat-breathing police officer who was seconds away from carting me off to jail. The officer proceeded to tell me that if I was taken to jail, my car would be impounded and my sons would be in the care of the state's social service agency because they would have no parental supervision without me.

I stood there on the side of the road helpless and desperate. I quietly prayed with passion, beseeching God to send something or someone to give me a lift. I needed someone to give my sons and me a ride home. I also needed someone else with a valid driver's license to drive my car.

At that moment I looked up to see a car passing by that appeared to be driven by Charles Mason. I threw my hands up in the air and jumped up and down in the hope that he would see me in his rearview mirror as he passed. He was approaching a red light. For a split second that instant hope for help seemed to vanish. I just knew Charles did not see me. If he had seen me, he probably didn't recognize me. Why would he recognize me? He hardly knew me.

Inside I silently screamed a cry for help. Then I noticed the brake lights were still applied, even though the traffic light had turned green. I noticed a turn signal and the car turned around! Sure enough I made contact with Charles. Like an angel on assignment, he was coming my way. Not only was he an angel on assignment, but he came with a posse of angels. Charles gave my sons and me a lift back to his house. Charles' friend, a very kind pastor who "happened" to be with him, drove my car to Charles' home. Then Babbie took my sons to school and took me to renew my insurance and to restore my driver's license! As I have heard someone say, "The Lord steps in just when we need Him most."

I sensed my neighbor's frustrations that day, and I thanked the Lord that Charles and I were not on the road so we could be there for him. As my mother has often said, "If it ain't one thing, it's another." You fix one thing, and something else breaks. You pay one bill, and another one comes due. You repair the car, and the furnace blows. Truly, it is always something. But I am reminded of John 16:33.

> Here on earth you will have many trials and sorrows; but cheer up, for I have overcome the world.
>
> —TLB

No matter how big by problem is, God is bigger.

FRUSTRATION IN THE BIBLE

There are so many people in the Bible who have walked the

road of frustration. We will take a look at a woman in Genesis 29 whose life was one big episode of disappointment. Her name was Leah.

Laban had two daughters, Leah, the older, and her younger sister, Rachel. Leah had weak and dull-looking eyes. Her spirit had no sparkle, and she was rather timid. Some say that Leah may have been short and frumpy. Others say that she was tall and gangly, with big feet. Maybe she had a lazy eye, causing her vision to be slightly impaired. However she looked, she just didn't measure up. She was always compared to her younger sister, Rachel.

Ah, Rachel. She was probably movie star material. She stood at just the right height, with a gorgeous figure and a glowing countenance. She was lively and happy, with a vivacious personality. She was the envy of every woman and the desire of every man—particularly one man named Jacob. He had his eye fixed and his heart set on marrying Rachel. Little did he know he'd have to wait a long while and pay a high price to have her hand in marriage. (See Genesis 29:16–23.)

When Jacob saw Rachel, it was love at first sight. He longed to have her for his wife, so he went to speak with Laban to ask for his daughter's hand in marriage. Laban spelled it out for Jacob, and Jacob agreed to Laban's requirements. He agreed to work for Laban for seven years. At the end of that seven-year period, Rachel would become his wife.

After Jacob had fulfilled the terms of his contract with Laban, Jacob said to Laban. "Give me my wife. My time is completed, and I want to lie with her" (Gen. 29:21). As custom would have it, on the evening of the wedding day when the marriage was to be consummated, the bride was veiled and the bride chamber was dark. The bride was brought in during the darkness of the evening. Jacob slept with her. But it was not until the next morning that Jacob found out that he had taken Leah and not Rachel.

Jacob was enraged! "What is this you have done to me? I served you for Rachel, didn't I? Why have you deceived me?" (v. 25).

Laban told Jacob that it was the custom to marry off the older daughter before the younger. Jacob had earlier tricked his father and robbed his brother, Esau, of the family blessing. The deceiver in the family had now been deceived. (See Genesis 27:14–38.) Jacob learned the hard way that what goes around comes around.

Can you imagine the anger and frustration that Jacob was feeling at that moment? Reluctantly, he agreed to work seven more years. After concluding Leah's bridal week, Laban also gave him Rachel. "Jacob lay with Rachel also, and he loved Rachel more than Leah" (Gen. 29:30). Because the custom was permitted in that day, Jacob took both Leah and Rachel as wives at the same time. This situation set the stage for a head-to-head competition between two sisters who had to share the same husband. Can you see a storm a-brewin' on the horizon? You know, just because something is accepted in the culture doesn't make it right.

Leah found herself in a very uncomfortable and frustrating predicament. As a result, she set out on a mission impossible. That mission was to win Jacob's love.

While winning Jacob's love was the ultimate goal, Leah would be content for the moment with his *appreciation*. Can't you just read Leah's thoughts, expressed or unexpressed? *Hey, Jacob. I'm a good wife. I cook your meals. I bear your children. I've saved all my love for you. Could you at least look this way? How about a little appreciation here?* Leah had to face the facts, and the truth hurts. Her husband loved another woman more than he loved her.

As I travel and minister all over the country, I hear countless stories of women who find themselves either in marriages or relationships where they feel unloved. This type of situation presents many women with the highest level of frustration and the lowest blow that life can deliver. Professional marriage and family therapists have told me that the number one external stressor is the death of a loved one. That's followed up by the betrayal of a loved one.

Leah's husband hadn't died. No, this was worse. Her husband was living, but he behaved as if she did not exist. Would you say that Leah was a candidate for frustration? It was as if Leah were dying a slow death. You may be in a situation right now where you have done all you know to do to gain your mate's attention. You've gone through many changes. You may have gotten pregnant, quit your job, changed your hairstyle, joined the gym, gone back to school—the list could go on and on—and still that has not been enough! Jesus sees your frustration and recognizes you right there in the midst of your pain. Isaiah 43:1 says, "Fear not, for I have redeemed you; I have summoned you by name; you are mine." Take comfort in the fact that Jesus knows what it is like to be rejected. Isaiah 53:3 says, "He was despised and rejected by men, a man of sorrows, and familiar with suffering." If you are experiencing rejection or sorrow or any other painful emotion, remember that Jesus has walked where you are walking. He knows how you feel.

In the Hebrew culture, when a parent named a child, within the name was a prayer or prophecy. The parents more or less petitioned God for what they believed or hoped would come forth from the life of that child. I find this extremely interesting when you look closely at the names Leah gave the children that she bore for Jacob.

Leah was certain that the way she would get Jacob to love her was to give him children. God blessed her womb, and she bore Jacob his first son, *Reuben* (meaning "God has noticed my trouble"). Then she said, "Jehovah has noticed my trouble—now my husband will love me" (Gen. 29:32, TLB). Leah was striving for Jacob's love and *attention*. She craved for him to notice her, to concentrate on her, to be interested in her.

All right. Let's get real for a moment. I think every married woman I know has said something like this to her husband: "If you want my attention in the bedroom, then don't ignore me in the kitchen!" In other words, don't act as if I don't exist all day, then cling to me like a magnet the moment we get into bed! Well, this was where Leah was living. Jacob wouldn't give Leah the time of day but was eager to sleep with her at night.

Leah was in trouble from the start. Let's recap. She was placed in a marriage by deception with a man who wanted someone else. To make matters worse, that someone else was her younger sister. It's clear. Jacob loved Rachel. He worked an additional seven years for Rachel while married to Leah. How do you think you would feel in a situation like that? I can imagine Leah felt quite lonely, unloved, unwanted and unnoticed.

Let me ask you a question. What is the opposite of love? You might say hatred. May I suggest to you that the opposite of love is not hatred? *The opposite of love is indifference.* Indifference says you do not exist. Indifference is to ignore. That is where Leah was living. Is that where you are living right now? Has your spouse, relatives, coworker or your church overlooked you? Are you feeling left out? There is someone who has had His eye on you before you were a gleam in your mother's eye. His name is Jesus. He never sleeps nor slumbers, and He is always watching over you. He sees you and has noticed your troubles.

Leah bore Jacob another son and named him *Simeon* (meaning "Jehovah heard"). She said, "Jehovah heard that I was unloved, and so he has given me another son" (v. 33, TLB). Leah was striving for Jacob's love and *acknowledgment*. To be *acknowledged* means to be recognized as genuine or valid. She wanted him to admit that he had heard her cry. She wanted to know that he heard her conversations whether she spoke a word or not. She wanted so desperately to have a husband who would be so in tune with her that he could tell what she needed without her even having to ask.

In my neighborhood, we say, "She wanted him to read her." Jacob was reading, to be sure. He was reading love sonnets to sister Rachel. Leah was the first to fill the family photo album with the pictures of little ones, because Rachel could not have children. Leah's house was full, but her heart was empty. She probably felt that she had no voice, no one to talk with and no one to listen. How many pillows will be wet with tears tonight because some husband or wife, son or daughter, boyfriend or girlfriend will lie down tonight feeling that no one is listening?

God will never put you on hold or ask you to leave a message.

Has anyone ever made you feel that you have nothing valuable to contribute, that you're not worth listening to? You can get in touch with God by using what I call God's phone number, *Jere-333*. That's Jeremiah 33:3. It says:

> Call to me and I will answer you and tell you great and unsearchable things you do not know.

Call on God. He will hear and answer your call. His line is never busy. He doesn't have call waiting. He'll never put you on hold or ask you to leave a message. But He longs to hear your voice and tell you about the wonderful plans He has for you.

So much of our activity is based on a need to be acknowledged. We go to great extents to get the one we love to recognize us. We may dress a certain way, buy a certain automobile, live in certain neighborhood or send our children to a certain school. All this is in an effort to be recognized and acknowledged. I know the story of a woman who knew her husband was having an affair with another woman. She did everything she knew to get her husband to return her love, including dressing like the other woman. This caused her husband to retreat all the more.

Again Leah strove to earn Jacob's approval by bearing him another son. She named her third son *Levi* (meaning "attachment"). This time she said, "Now at last my husband will become attached to me, because I have borne him three sons" (Gen. 29:34). Leah longed for Jacob's affection. *Affection* means a moderate feeling or emotion, a tender attachment, a fondness. Have you ever gone looking for love in all the wrong places just for a little affection? It's funny; we all long to belong. That's why we join this club and that organization. We even get married to meet that need. Then if that need is not fulfilled, real loneliness sets in.

Real loneliness is when you have joined something, but it has not joined you! It's like being all alone in a great big crowd. It's like being in a house with a spouse, but you're nothing more than roommates. Leah was joined to Jacob, but he was not joined to her. He had no *feelings of affection* for her. He did not want to be with her just to be with her. His heart did not skip a beat when he heard her voice or saw her coming. Can you feel Leah's pain? Look closely, my friend. Do you see a pattern here? Do you recognize a vicious cycle in this relationship? I've heard it said more than once that insanity is doing the same thing over and over again expecting different results. Leah finally realized that nothing she did was going to earn

Jacob's approval. Therefore she came to an end. But this was not the end for Leah. This was the very place where she should have begun.

Leah bore Jacob a fourth son, *Judah* (meaning "Praise"). Now she said, "Now I will praise Jehovah!" (v. 35, TLB). And then she stopped having children.

Leah desired to please Jacob. But she wanted to please God more. There are times in our lives when we reach the end of our efforts. We have looked in every direction for the answer. The only direction left to look is up. Leah looked up for her answer and found it. She finally put aside her frustration and began to praise God. She looked up and stopped having children in an effort to gain her husband's approval. She ceased her striving—at least for the moment. Leah was a slow learner.

Leah gave Jacob more children. He also had children with his wife Rachel and his substitute wives, Zilpah and Bilhah. This family and their children were plagued with anger, bitterness and jealousy, and it reaped bitter results in the lives of their children. Fighting and disagreement were common occurrences between Leah's and Rachel's children. It's unfortunate that children often pay the price for their parent's mistakes.

Personal identity, dignity and esteem come from God and God alone.

Whose approval are you seeking right now? Is it the approval of your spouse, children, boss or a friend? Have you exhausted all your efforts, energies and resources? How many times have we desired from someone else that which we can only get from God? Or perhaps we have desired from someone else that which they were incapable of giving.

Jesus never felt that He had to earn the approval of anyone. His will and desire were only to please the Father. You and I should never seek the accolades of people. Draw close to God, and He will draw close to you. Develop a close attachment to Him, and allow Him to fill you with His Spirit, presence and affection. A lifestyle of prayer and study of God's Word is an excellent foundation for receiving and distributing godly affection.

Personal identity, dignity and esteem come from God and God alone. Get to the place where you live your life for an audience of ONE—God Himself. In Galatians 1:10 Paul states, "You can see that I am not trying to please you by sweet talk and flattery; no, I am trying to please God. If I were still trying to please men I could not be Christ's servant" (TLB).

If you see yourself in this story about Leah, I suggest you pick up where Leah left off. After trying for so long to please Jacob, the object of her affections, she finally realized, if only for a moment, that she must no longer place her focus on Jacob, but rather on the Lord. You, like Leah, can finally find fulfillment in the love of a God who is pleased with you just the way you are. You don't have to lose weight to be appreciated. You don't have to change your hair color to get some acknowledgment. You don't have to get a facelift to get affection. You, my friend, are already accepted in the Beloved.

This story is a classic case of misplaced affections. As long as we look to people to fill the gaping void that only God can fill, we will forever be empty. As long as we hold others responsible to meet our deepest need to be loved, we will always be left wanting. My friend Lana Bateman is the lead intercessor for the Women of Faith Conference, the largest women's conference in the nation. I frequently have the privilege of singing in the conferences. Lana said something once that reminded me of the way we, like Leah, live by cheating ourselves out of the rich inheritance God intended for us to have. She said, "Don't get caught bankrupt while standing in the vaults of Heaven. It's a picture of what we think we have compared to what we *really* have."

Leah's story brings home so much. But this one thing we must learn from it. Only God can love you to the point that you are truly satisfied. No husband can love you like that. A house full of children won't ease the pain. Only Jesus can heal you where you hurt. Only He can love you deeply, richly and fully.

Do not worry, saying, "What shall we eat?" or "What shall we drink?" or "What shall we wear?" ... your heavenly Father knows that you need them. But seek first his kingdom and his righteousness, and all these things will be given to you as well.

—MATTHEW 6:31–33

CHAPTER 9

Faith

Your Fretting

I N THE EARLY eighties, I was enjoying my job as a music teacher in middle school. God began to open doors for me to sing around the city of Atlanta, so I was also making concert appearances one or two Sundays a month. Little by little my singing calendar became so full that it began to compete with my day job. One time I sang in Dallas, Texas, on a Sunday, then drove all night to get back to Marietta, Georgia, for work on Monday morning.

Challenges and conflicts arose. I did my best to juggle my responsibilities as a wife, mother, teacher and singer and still have a life. By 1984, I was being pulled in all directions. Something had to give somewhere. I could not continue working at this pace if I wanted to keep my health and my sanity. I struggled over my choices. Talking it over with my husband helped, but he left the final decision up to me. Should I continue to teach, or should I leave the classroom to follow my dream to become a gospel singer?

I talked it over with God. The answer did not seem to be clear. If I continued with this unrealistic schedule, I would definitely be overcommitted, ineffective, stressed and exhausted. If I retired from my job as a teacher, then I'd lose my health and retirement benefits. Our children were very young, and that was a very real concern. Charles had just started his own business and was not making enough money to buy expensive healthcare coverage. I labored in prayer over this situation.

Finally the time came when I had to make a decision. The county board of education had sent out forms requesting that I let them know of my intent to return to the classroom in preparation for the upcoming school year. My principal would have to have my answer a few days after I received the form. I weighed my options. I laid my requests before the Lord. I waited for an answer.

One evening a friend of ours dropped by our home for a visit. She brought a precious couple with her to meet Charles and me. The gentleman was an evangelist who lived in the Atlanta area. We were honored to meet this man of God and his wife. We talked for a while. Before they left, the very kind man asked if there were any concerns I had that we needed to pray about.

I shared with all of them that it was my desire to step out in faith into the music ministry. I told them that I was seeking God for an answer. I felt I was running out of time, and I needed to know God's will on the matter. My concerns had turned to worries. Charles told them that he supported me in this, but we both felt that it was not wise for me to quit my job and leave our growing family with no healthcare. I told them that we needed to hear from God concerning our next step.

That brother prayed a powerful prayer of faith. Then he told Charles and me that he and his wife would pay for our healthcare for the next year! That precious brother never knew that the Intent to Return form was due on my principal's desk the following morning. As much as I loved the teaching profession, I retired in 1984. That was almost twenty years ago. God has truly been faithful over the years. My husband continues to remind me, though, that I didn't quit teaching. My classroom just got bigger.

I wish I could say that during the time that I was waiting on God for an answer, I didn't have one moment of worry. When I didn't hear from God, I waited. I wondered. And yes, I even worried. But I learned a tremendous lesson during that season in my life. I learned that worry serves absolutely no purpose in the life of a believer. God already had a plan, and His plan worked, as it always does, in a beautiful way for my good.

> *Only God can see the beginning and the end at the same time.*

The definition of *worry* is a feeling of uneasiness, anxiousness or dread. It means to be overly concerned, troubled or fearful, usually over things that never happen. Worrying about something that may never happen is like paying interest on money you may never borrow. Have you ever wondered, *My mother had cancer; will I get cancer? Will I have enough money to send my children to college? Will my husband still love me if I gain weight? Will my child be safe while away at school? Will my money be secure in my retirement account?* Do you rehash these questions or scenarios—and others—over and over in your mind?

The headlines in today's newspapers are enough to freeze the average person in her tracks. School violence, economic issues, health-related news, the threat of war, the energy crisis, the rising divorce rate, child kidnappings and sniper shootings are huge threats that seem to loom over our world like monstrous dragons. But worrying over these things will not change their outcome. The future, my friend, is not ours to worry about. It is out of our control. But God does know every detail of your future. The future belongs to Him. Only God can see the beginning and the end at the same time.

I heard Dr. David Jeremiah tell the story of Mickey Rivers, an outfielder who played for the Texas Rangers. Mickey had a simple way of looking at life as it related to worry. He said, "Ain't no sense worryin'. If you have no control over something, ain't no sense worryin'—you have no control over it anyway. If you do have control, ain't no sense worryin'. So either way, there ain't no sense worryin'."[1]

PRAYER IS BETTER THAN WORRY

I think Mickey Rivers had it down just about right. Don't get into the habit of worrying about anything. Not even about your health, your marriage, your family or your safety. Not about anything. That is what Philippians 4:6 tells us.

> Do not be anxious about anything, but in everything,
> by prayer and petition, with thanksgiving, present
> your requests to God.

What a powerful truth that is. Don't worry about anything, but pray about everything. Nothing is worth worrying about. Everything is worth praying about. So then, turn your worries into prayers.

Worry is a thief. And if you allow it, worry will let your tomorrow steal from your today. Worry will rob you of your rest, take your joy, consume your energy and preoccupy your thoughts. Arthur S. Roche said, "Worry is a thin stream of fear trickling through the mind. If encouraged, it cuts a channel into which all other thoughts are drained."[2]

You are commanded not to worry because God knows every intricate detail about you. He will meet your needs. The Bible calls worry a sin, and it speaks much on the subject. Jesus addresses the issue in Matthew 6.

> Therefore I tell you, do not worry about your life, what you will eat or drink; or about your body, what you will wear. Is not life more important than food, and the body more important than clothes? Look at the birds of the air; they do not sow or reap or store away in barns, and yet your heavenly Father feeds them. Are you not much more valuable than they? Who of you by worrying can add a single hour to his life?
>
> And why do you worry about clothes? See how the lilies of the field grow. They do not labor or spin. Yet I tell you that not even Solomon in all his splendor was dressed like one of these. If that is how God clothes the grass of the field, which is here today and tomorrow is thrown into the fire, will he not much more clothe you, O you of little faith? So do not worry, saying, "What shall we eat?" or "What shall we drink?" or "What shall we wear?" For the pagans run after all these things, and your heavenly Father knows that you need them. But seek first his kingdom and his righteousness, and all these things will be given to you as well. Therefore do not worry about tomorrow, for tomorrow will worry about itself. Each day has enough trouble of its own.
>
> —MATTHEW 6:25–34

In this passage of Scripture Jesus assures us that the same God who gave us life is able to take care of that life. Supplying our needs is God's job. When we try to do God's job, we invite worry to enter our hearts. Jesus wants us to know that worry is *work*. Worry works as a distraction to get your mind off God's promises and off your purpose. Like a dripping faucet, it will begin to wear you down, causing you to weaken. It takes constant effort and energy to worry.

One dictionary definition says that *worry* means to weary. It leaves you tired and burned out because you are more likely to lose sleep when you worry. You will find that worry creates nothing but more to worry about. If you have been caught up in the trap of worry, you also are probably anxious and exhausted. Winston Churchill commented on the life of an old man who confessed on his deathbed that he had encountered a lot of trouble in his life, most of which never happened.

Worry is a futile task of fruitless thoughts. It is a brutal slave driver. Wouldn't you rather cast all your cares on the Lord and wipe your hands of the whole thing? You can, you know. Look at the birds of the air and the lilies of the field. They don't worry about where their next meal is going to come from. They don't worry about the weather conditions—whether it will rain or the sun will shine. Have you ever seen a sparrow die of starvation? Have you ever seen an ugly lily? Neither have I. Jesus says we are much more valuable than they are.

Jesus is adamant in His teaching. Verse 27 in the New King James Version says, "Which of you by worrying can add one cubit to his stature?" As much as we'd like that to be so, it's not possible. Most of the people on my husband's side of the family are not tall people. Charles, who stands at about five foot eight inches, once showed me a picture of him that was taken in the sixties. I was curious as to why he stood taller than usual in the picture. He told me it was because he was wearing platform shoes. In the picture, he appeared to be almost six feet tall. Platform shoes work wonders when you want to appear taller. But at the end of the day, they end up in the closet. The Bible says worrying won't make you taller. And it won't add anything to your life span. It is of no value. It is *worthless*.

You pay a high price when you live a life full of anxiety. As a matter of fact, worry is extremely unhealthy. Doctors will tell you that worry is often the precursor to high blood pressure, stroke and heart disease. Surgeon Charles Horace Mayo, cofounder of the Mayo Clinic, said, "Worry affects the circulation, the heart, the glands, the whole nervous system. I have never known a man who died from overwork, but many who have died from doubt."[3]

Jesus knows that having a fretful attitude is a wasteful exercise. He knows that it contributes nothing; it only takes away the peace that God promised He would give you. Worry multiplies nothing—no joys, no pleasures, no hopes or dreams. It only divides your mind as you find yourself going back and forth, back and forth, rehearsing your problems. It causes you to be double minded. The Bible tells us that a double-minded man is unstable in everything he does (James 1:8).

Never forget that worry is *worthless*. It is never helpful, only harmful. Worry is like getting into your car, shifting to neutral and continually revving up the motor. You'll expend lots of effort and energy, but you will go nowhere. You will just get all heated up over nothing. Why not put your time and energy into something productive? God has gifted you to carry out an assignment that will glorify His kingdom, encourage others along the way and bring you great joy while doing it. You don't have time to worry. You have work to do!

Jesus wants you to know that worry is not becoming to a Christian. Matthew 6:32 says that worrying about food, drink and clothing is what pagans do. In other words, worry is *worldly*. The shopping malls are filled with people who are worrying over what to eat, what to drink and what to wear.

Do you see a connection here? The very things that God tells us not to worry about are the main things that fuel the retail industry. I am not saying, "Don't spend money at the mall." But often things that we want, not things that we need, perpetuate our shopping habits. People who don't know the Lord worry about such things. Children of God confidently hide the Word in their hearts so they don't fall into sin.

Here is a great promise to remember: "Many are the woes of the wicked, but the LORD'S unfailing love surrounds the man who trusts in him" (Ps. 32:10). Worry will lead you into disobedience. It will convince you to spend money you don't have. That will only create more worry. Worry will cause you to question God, not trust Him. Live your life one day at a time. Don't fret over yesterday. Don't worry about tomorrow. Live only for today. Think about this. Sorrow looks back. Worry looks ahead. But faith looks up.

Worry is worthless.

One day while preparing dinner, I was sharing a prayer request with a friend who was visiting our home. My prayer request had turned into a gripe session as I went on and on about my situation. I grumbled as I reached into the spice cabinet to grab the salt. I mumbled as I reached in again to get the pepper. I sputtered as I reached in once again for the garlic powder. As I retrieved the garlic powder, another spice toppled out of the cabinet, just grazing me on the head as it fell to the floor. As I bent over to pick the jar up from the floor, my friend and I blurted out with belly laughs. It was a jar of mustard seed!

As I've said before, I'm a slow learner. God sometimes has to draw me pictures. I got the message loud and clear. Don't worry; pray. Don't complain; pray. Don't be anxious; pray.

That incident reminded my friend who was visiting our home of a mustard-seed faith situation in his own life where he needed to believe that God would take care of his every need.

My friend Kenn had resigned from his job as an associate music minister to go into music evangelism as a full-time vocation. He and his wife, Angela, were living in New Orleans, where they were enrolled in the New Orleans Theological Seminary.

I'll let Kenn tell the story.

> Angela and I were extremely excited about this new venture. We believed God was directing our steps, and we felt confident that God would meet our needs because we had concerts booked several months in advance. It was comforting to look at our concert calendar and see many Sunday night concerts booked. But in the middle of our confident season, a storm arose. The storm came by way of the telephone.
>
> During the following three-week period, every concert that we had was canceled. Every one of them just fell through. Every pastor that had confirmed a concert had a legitimate reason for canceling that concert. "Our church is in the middle of a building fund, and we need to tighten our financial belt." "Our church had a fire." Another church called to say, "Our pastor has died." We could not believe that in such a short time, our whole ministry seemed to fall apart right before our eyes.
>
> I began to worry. I even began to second-guess our call to evangelism. "We have missed God," I told my wife.
>
> My wife said firmly to me. "No. This is a test. God is testing us to see what we are made of. I'm not going to tell you what Job's wife told him, which was, 'Curse God and die.' Instead, I'll remind you that this is a test from God. He wants to see what we are made of."
>
> Our cupboards were bare. Rent was due. Bills were piling up. We were flat broke. No money was coming

in. The next step in the process was to call our parents and ask them for money. You can call it *pride*, but I just didn't want to do that. That was the last resort. I'd wait a few more days before I called them.

New Orleans is known for Mardi Gras, a wild party atmosphere where people get drunk in the streets and party until the wee hours of the morning. During Mardi Gras, there is a huge parade where people throw colorful beads from their floats as they ride by. People along the parade route collect as many strands of beads as they can, believing it will bring them good fortune.

Seminary students look at this holiday as an opportunity to witness for Christ in the streets. We were invited to join our friends, but my wife and I refused to go near the Mardi Gras festivities. We didn't like the environment—not even to witness. We just didn't want to be down there. Because of that, our friends played a practical joke on us by decorating the outside of our apartment door with hundreds upon hundreds of Mardi Gras beads. I can remember it clearly—my wife could not even open the door because of the mountain of beads that blocked our apartment's entrance.

Rather than pick up the beads and throw them in the trash, she said, "I can use these beads to make jewelry." My wife is very creative. Sometimes she makes earrings and things to give to friends or to sell at craft shows. So I bagged the beads and put them in the closet and thought no more about them.

Every morning I jogged around the block, near the New Orleans Quarter. One day while jogging I saw a sign in a store window that read, "We buy beads—a penny a bead." Now that may mean nothing to you, but to my growling stomach, it meant food! My jog turned into a full gallop as I ran home to tell my wife the good news. We counted every bead. There were exactly 1,127 beads, which meant $11.27 worth of groceries. We took the beads to the store and redeemed them for cash. Immediately we went food shopping. We ate well for an entire week on just $11.27. Almost every day one of our neighbors would unexpectedly drop by with more food in tow. Money showed up out of nowhere with our name on it. We never shared our need with anyone, but God knew!

You have heard of having the faith of a mustard seed ...well, God gave us the faith of a mustard bead! What a great lesson we learned that day. "Trust in the LORD with all your heart and lean not on your own understanding; in all your ways acknowledge him, and he will make your paths straight" (Prov. 3:5–6). God was testing my wife and me to see what we were made of.

I came to this conclusion about testing. In the world we learn the lesson, then we take the test. In God's classroom of faith, we take the test, then we learn the lesson. That's why we have to walk by faith. The tests come first, and the answers come later. Regardless of what stage of testing you are in, trust God at every intersection.

I once heard the following lyrics from a little lady from Mississippi. She had a lot of insight about faith. Listen to her powerful words:

> You don't have to call the neighbor down the street
> Or tell the grocer that you don't have food to eat.
> If there's a need that must be met,
> God will answer, don't forget
> He will fix it;
> The answer is on your knees.[4]

Her words remind me that if a care is small enough to be made into a burden, then it is big enough to be made into a prayer. Life is too long to worry. Pray instead. Life is too short to worry. Pray instead.

Let's review a bit.

- Worry is work.
- Worry is worthless.
- Worthy is worldly.

Don't worry about anything. Don't worry about yesterday and all of its cares and regrets. If the past were significant to God, His name would be *I Was*. Don't fret over tomorrow and all of its unnecessary concerns. If the future were a concern to God, His name would be *I Will Be*. Today is all you have. Treasure it as a priceless gift from God. Allow Him to meet your needs moment by moment, day by day. For that is where you will find God. That is why He is called *I AM*. Let go of whatever it is you're holding on to. Give it to God. As Kenn experienced, Mardi Gras beads are worthless, only plastic.

Today is all you have.
Treasure it as a priceless
gift from God.

OK, they're worth a penny. But the treasures of God are priceless! Find the faith to trust God for today. Are you holding on to the plastic beads of whatever your situation is, when, all the time, God has already worked it out? Open your hand, and drop the worthless beads, my friend. You'll find the faith to let go and let God have His way.

These commandments that I give you today are to be upon your hearts. Impress them on your children. Talk about them when you sit at home and when you walk along the road, when you lie down and when you get up. Tie them as symbols on your hands and bind them on your foreheads. Write them on the doorframes of your houses and on your gates.

—DEUTERONOMY 6:6–9

CHAPTER 10

Faith

Your Family

M Y ROLE AS a parent is changing by the minute. It seemed like only yesterday that our youngest son, Chaz, was entering kindergarten. I remember the day Charles and I drove him to school. We walked him to his class. We introduced him to his teacher. We found his seat. We assured him that he would be fine. *He* was fine. *We* were basket cases. The teacher had to escort us to the classroom door. We left in tears. We ended up consoling each other over coffee and cinnamon rolls at the local coffee shop. Charles doesn't even drink coffee. He had two cups. Chaz is now on his way to college. He is on the edge of the nest. He is testing his wingspan and is ready to take flight.

Time flies when you're raising a family. It doesn't seem like that long ago that our oldest son, Jerry, was a toddler, sitting in the middle of the kitchen floor in the middle of his own stainless steel band. My best pots and pans and a set of wooden spoons were turned into a bass drum, a snare drum and a ride cymbal with two of the finest drumsticks a two-year-old could ask for. A fine percussionist and an audio engineer today, Jerry is all grown up and is married to Jessica, a precious young lady.

If you're a mother, then you know that motherhood is a huge

job. But somebody has to do it, so it might as well be you. The job description for mothers is long term and is not for the faint-hearted. It is only for those who are willing to work long hours and be on call around the clock, including nights and weekends. You must have excellent communication and problem-solving skills. No experience is necessary. You will learn everything you need to know on a continuous basis. If you don't have a particular skill, you'll learn it when you get there.

You must be willing to be hated, at least temporarily, until someone needs five dollars. Travel is required. You must be willing to go on field trips, including overnight camping trips at old Baptist campgrounds. An occasional 2 A.M. visit to the nearby hospital emergency room is to be expected. You must be willing to accept technical challenges and be available to make last-minute runs to the drug store on Sunday night for neon-colored poster board, and then assist in making collages that are due on Monday morning. You pay all expenses, including wages and compensation. You must offer frequent raises, bonuses and paid vacations. Your benefits will not include health, dental or life insurance. You will receive no pension or reimbursements for tuition. But you will receive a lifetime supply of free hugs and kisses and endless possibilities for life enrichment.

If you are a mother of young children, take courage. I know that raising children is not easy. I can't begin to count the number of diapers I've changed, noses I've wiped and skinned knees and elbows I've bandaged. I'd be a very rich woman if I had a dollar for every baseball, football and basketball game I've attended. I've played with my children, lectured them, laughed with them, prayed for them and just about pulled my hair out because of them. And in return, they have brought to our home sidesplitting laughter, toothless grins, parental pride, endless joy and lots of prom pictures.

Then one day I wake up, and the next thing I know, I'm a grandmother. If you had asked me in the spring of last year if I liked the color pink, I would have said, "Absolutely, positively no. I think pink looks great on ladies with fair skin and blond hair, but it washes my complexion out. I don't think pink does anything at all to enhance my dark hair and natural suntan." But in the spring of this year, I became the grandmother of a beautiful, bouncing, baby girl. I must tell you—*the whole world is pink.* My car now makes sudden turns into the Babies R Us store in an effort to find the latest pink frocks with matching pink socks. From the top of her head with the cute little pink bows, right down to the pink shoes on her cute little toes, my, she is pretty in pink.

At first, the idea of becoming a grandmother took some getting used to. I just didn't think I was mentally ready to be anybody's grandmother. I mean, I'm a jet-setter, and I couldn't imagine a little one calling me *Meemaw, Nanna* or *Granny.* But then my granddaughter was born. In the delivery room on the night when she made her grand entrance into the world, the nurse placed that precious bundle of love in my arms after she had her very first bath. Then it hit me like a ton of bricks. Through the tears and out of my mouth came the words, "Come to Meemaw. Come to your Nanna. Come to Granny. I don't care what you call me, just come to me!" It was love at first sight, and I have been deliriously in love with her ever since.

The next morning, I was basking in the idea that I was somebody's grandmother. However, I admitted to my husband that I really didn't think I was old enough to be anybody's grandmother. Then I put my feet on the floor. My feet hurt from walking around the huge arena the day before in high heels. I had sung in Shreveport, Louisiana, at a women's conference. My daughter-in-law had gone into labor before I left, so I knew I'd better beat it back to Atlanta with haste. I caught the first flight out of Shreveport and rushed right to the hospital to welcome my precious granddaughter into the world. When I arose the next morning, my feet were tired and achy from all the running around I had done on the previous day.

I decided to try a new pain reliever. The safety cap seemed a lot trickier to remove and the small print explaining the dosage seemed to be a lot smaller than usual. The previous day had been long and the evening at the hospital had been emotionally draining. And it showed when I looked at myself in the mirror. The circles under my eyes appeared deeper and darker than usual. I had been having some challenges with my hair, so I had started to wear the kind of hair that you put on in the morning and take off at night and lay on the dresser. I must have laid my hair by the front door, because I couldn't find it! I finally started getting it together. I got dressed. I put on my white cotton socks and some soft-soled shoes. I donned my reading glasses and took a couple of pain relievers for my aching feet. I dabbed a little wrinkle cream on the bags under my eyes. Then I finally located my hair. Completely dressed, I looked in the mirror and exclaimed to myself, "Think again, girlfriend. You *are* old enough to be somebody's grandmother."

You know, you can see grandmothers coming. We're the ones with the purse full of photographs. If you've ever been held hostage by a grandmother, you know the feeling: "Here is grandbaby sitting up. Here is grandbaby lying down. Here is grandbaby laughing. And here is grandbaby crying." Twenty pictures later, you're still trying to come up with compliments. The only one you can think of is, "Now, that's a baby!" You're wishing you'd never laid eyes on the woman. Well, beware. I have a purse full of photos, and I'm coming to a city near you!

I am aware, more than ever, of the importance and the responsibility of passing my faith along to the generations who come behind me. I look at our youngest son, who is a fine musician, and I pray that he will use his gifts for the encouragement of God's people and the glory of God's kingdom. He is a student, but I pray that he will represent Christ well on the campus and in his music.

Then I look at our oldest son, who is a young husband and a fine new papa. My heart swells with bittersweet emotion as he holds his little girl, and I whisper, "O God, I pray that we have taught them Your precepts well. May the precious seeds of our sweet faith in Jesus Christ sustain them and their families and bring forth much fruit for Your kingdom. Thank You, God, that You are faithful. I pray Your promises from Isaiah 55:11 over them, that *Your word shall not return void, but it will accomplish that which You please. It shall prosper in the thing for which You sent it.*"

> *I am aware, more than ever, of the importance and the responsibility of passing my faith along to the generations who come behind me.*

My family's history consists of five generations of preachers and pastors that I know of. My great-grandfather, my grandfather, my father, my oldest brother and his son were, and are, preachers and pastors. Now I see why I felt as if I had little choice but to serve God with my heart and with my vocation.

I tried as best as I could to become a popular R&B singer. When I was in college, periodically I sang in clubs around town. Every time I darkened the door of a nightclub or bar, I sensed the Holy Spirit's conviction in my heart so strongly that I could not enjoy myself. Although I was an adult, I feared that someone would recognize me and that the word would get back to my parents. I was a young Christian and the pianist for my father's church. Although I was out on my own, I never wanted it to be said that somebody saw Reverend Wade's daughter in a nightclub. I know beyond a shadow of a doubt that the prayers of my mother were sustaining me at that critical time in my life.

I realize now that just because my children are grown does not mean that my responsibility to pray for them has ended. I know I must pray for them now more than ever. Passing my faith along has taken on a whole new meaning as I see our sons getting older and our family increasing. Oh, how I want to be the mirror image of Christ as I influence my little grand-daughter to love the Lord.

ONE MOTHER'S GODLY EXAMPLE

One woman whose life exhibited such a godly example for her children was Susanna Wesley. Between 1690 and 1709, she birthed nineteen children. Her fifteenth child, John, was the founder of the Methodist movement. Her son Charles, her eighteenth child, penned some of the church's most beloved hymns. From their birth, Susanna was concerned about the spiritual welfare of all her children. On Sunday nights, she packed their home with as many as two hundred neighbors who had come to hear her preach the gospel. She taught her children as well. They carried their spiritual heritage on into their adult lives, for all of her children were truly devout. She was strict in teaching her children at home. Not only did she teach them precepts from the Bible, but six hours a day for twenty years she instilled in them a love for learning.

Susanna Wesley was a wife and mother who knew extreme hardship. Her husband, Samuel, did not manage the family's finances well and was put in a debtor's prison. Susanna endured the entire responsibility for the support of her family, teaching and caring for the children and caring for their farm animals. During those years of raising a family, she suffered through numerous sicknesses. Their home burned to the ground. Several of her children were afflicted with chronic ailments, and several died. Throughout all the difficult circumstances, Susanna practiced what she preached and never wavered in her faith.

> *This is the essence of faith—to be able to see a thing before it actually comes to pass.*

She instilled hope into the lives of each of her children and believed in their dreams. For example, although Susanna's husband was a minister, he discouraged young John in his quest to become a preacher. It was Susanna who encouraged John to follow God's leading and enter into the preaching ministry.

John and Charles Wesley later left England and went to Savannah, Georgia, as missionaries. They would return to London where Susanna would accompany John on his trips to preach to as many as twenty thousand people. Charles, a

preacher as well, was becoming well known for his sacred hymn writing.

Known as the Mother of Methodism, Susanna Wesley lived to bring about the best in her children. In a letter, she encouraged her son Samuel, also a preacher, with these words:

> Consider well what a separation from the world, what a purity, what devotion, what exemplary virtue, are required in those who are to guide others to glory. I would advise you to arrange your affairs by a certain method, by which means you will learn to improve every precious moment. Begin and end the day with Him who is the Alpha and Omega, and if you really experience what it is to love God, you will redeem all the time you can for His more immediate service.[1]

Susanna Wesley invested so much good into the lives of her children. But there are three things I want to note.

She taught her children to be people of great *vision*.

In Proverbs 29:18 we read: "Where there is no vision, the people perish" (KJV). Almost three hundred years after their births, John and Charles Wesley would not only have an impact on the Methodist Church, but on the church at large, world wide. This is the essence of faith—to be able to see a thing before it actually comes to pass. Susanna Wesley excelled at this and taught her children that vision only comes from God. Before a task can be done well, a well-honed vision must precede it.

The Wesley children were taught to possess *virtue*.

Few of our children today are taught to be people of quality, merit and moral character. In fact, it seems that everything is being done to erase morality in our country. We cannot depend upon our government to teach virtues to our children.

Goodness, integrity, respect, honesty, kindness and responsibility first have to be taught at home.

Our children must be taught that the measure of a man is not summed up in what he possesses, but by what good he does with that which he possesses. I heard a frightening statistic recently that should challenge every parent to spend more time teaching his or her children the good things that God has promised. Does this shock you as much as it does me? The average parent spends very little quality time with her child. A school-aged child spends an average of forty hours a week in school and twenty hours in front of the television or other secular media. But that same child spends, on the average, *only one hour of quality time a week with a parent.* Is it any wonder, in many cases, that instead of our children possessing character, a character is what they have become? The first classroom that every child should experience is the one at home. We must be diligent to teach our children that God rewards those whose hearts are upright and blameless before Him.

The Wesley children were taught they were of tremendous *value.*

In the Wesley home, each child knew in his heart that he was of tremendous *value* to his parents, to society and to God. We hear so much talk today about self-esteem. I believe self-esteem and worth begin to be achieved when a child is taught to realize that he is of priceless worth to God. That possessive love of God leaps off the page as the Word of the Lord speaks to the prophet Jeremiah:

> Before I formed you in the womb I knew you,
> before you were born, I set you apart.
>
> —JEREMIAH 1:5

It is no secret that the devil is after the hearts and minds of our children. Do not leave the rearing of your children to secular education or to the television. Step up to your active role and God-given responsibility to:

> Train up a child in the way he should go [and in keeping with his individual gift or bent], and when he is old he will not depart from it.
>
> —PROVERBS 22:6, AMP

My own mother, Georgie Wade, raised five children and instilled in all of us vision, virtue and value. She believed that the principles of the Bible were not only taught, but caught. We were raised in the fear and admonition of the Lord, but our parents lived it out before us. Our mother taught us to love God and to serve Him with our hands and with our hearts. Our home was always filled with music and particularly the sound of her beautiful voice. In bringing us up, she was loving and generous, but she had no problem laying down the law—God's and man's. When it came to discipline, she often had to do the hard thing. When it came to praying for us, I remember hearing her say once that if we ever did anything that was outside of the will of God, she would pray, "Let them get caught."

Above all, Susanna Wesley and Georgie Wade both taught their children to live a life of praise. Here are some words to one of Charles Wesley's most beloved hymns:

> O for a thousand tongues to sing
> My great Redeemer's praise,
> The glories of my God and King,
> The triumphs of His grace!
>
> Jesus, the name that calms my fears,
> That bids my sorrows cease,
> 'Tis music in the sinner's ears;
> 'Tis life and health and peace.[2]

That powerful hymn has outlived Charles Wesley by over two hundred years. Those words were penned in the mid-1700s, and we are still singing them today.

Someday after you and I are long gone, hopefully, our children and grandchildren will speak of us with fond memories. Maybe they will compliment the way we cooked or dressed. Or maybe they will comment on what a great friend we were. But may it be said of us, the highest compliment, that we were women of prayer and praise who loved God and our families and trained our children well.

Here are some of my own words, which I wrote in response to the rich heritage that I have in my family. As you read them, I believe you will dare to leave a legacy of faith for your children and grandchildren for generations to come.

> The patriarchs of old
> The saints that now are gone
> To their great reward
> Held fast to the struggle
> Persistent through the years
> Forging through their fears
> They fought to change
> Their world for the sake
> Of the gospel
> May their love for Jesus
> Never go unnoticed
> May they spur us on to all
> That lies before us.
>
> This heritage of faith
> This legacy of love
> We must pass to our daughters
> Hand down to our sons
> We must raise the standard
> High and proclaim

The Name of Christ
That others may know the way
And this heritage of faith.[3]

If you have a godly heritage, thank God for it. If you don't have a family history with God at the root of your family tree, let it start with you. Your faith in Christ will make up for lost time and make all the difference for your family's future—now and for eternity.

Consider it pure joy, my brothers, when—
ever you face trials of many kinds, because
you know that the testing of your faith
develops perseverance. Perseverance must
finish its work so that you may be mature
and complete, not lacking anything.

—JAMES 1:2–4

CHAPTER 11

Faith
the Fundamentals

IN COMPLETING ONE'S education, it's not only the *IQ* that matters, but the *I will* that contributes to a passing grade. Just as life's greatest lessons are learned in the classroom, the fundamentals of trusting and believing God are honed in the classroom of faith. With the Bible as the textbook for living and the Holy Spirit as the Instructor who guides us into all truth, the best students are the ones who learn from adversity to pass life's greatest tests.

If you are somewhere in your forties or older, then you probably remember the days of black and white television. I was very young then, but those days I remember well. No cable TV. No remote control. No satellite. No high-definition television or informercials. Our viewing selection consisted of only three network stations. Reception was good most times. A rabbit-ear antenna perched atop the television set would do a good job of bringing the picture into focus. If all else failed, a bit of aluminum foil wrapped around the antenna's ends would act as a conductor. This would help to sharpen the picture, particularly if someone gingerly held on to that piece of aluminum foil with one hand while holding the other hand in the air. Television stations signed off at midnight with a word of inspiration and the playing of the National Anthem. As they say, "Those were the days."

One significant memory concerning television in the sixties was a test administered by the Emergency Broadcasting System. Normal programming was interrupted, and an emblem would appear on the screen, followed by a long tone. Then viewers would hear these words; "This is a test of the Emergency Broadcasting System. This is a test. This is only a test." The announcer would proceed to tell viewers what to do in case of a local or national emergency.

Likewise, the Word of God tells us that the Christian can be prepared for times of crisis. The Bible tells us that our faith will be tested. *When,* not *if,* we encounter those various trials, these trials are a test of our faith. If we look at difficulty through the eyes of faith, we will find that God causes us to benefit from times of testing.

Although we may not welcome tough times, the Book of James says it is possible to look at trials with an attitude of joy.

> Consider it pure joy, my brothers, whenever you face trials of many kinds, because you know that the testing of your faith develops perseverance. Perseverance must finish its work so that you may be mature and complete, not lacking anything.
>
> —JAMES 1:2–4

As a student in the classroom of faith, you will find yourself facing a battery of difficulties. Life's trials are inevitable. No one can escape them. The Book of Job shows us that life on earth is warfare. We all have to deal with tribulation. Oftentimes it comes as a result of our own lack of judgment. At other times, adversity comes out of the clear blue. More than likely, you are facing some kind of trial at this very moment. But you can be assured that these circumstances are not working against you, but for you. The outcome will depend on your attitude. Remember, this is a test; this is only a test.

> *If we look at difficulty through the eyes of faith, we will find that God causes us to benefit from times of testing.*

When it comes to taking and passing life's tests, you should know that you're not the only one who has faced hardship. Everyone has to face life's examinations. Tests are something we all must encounter.

THE TEST IS NORMAL

If you keep on living, if you don't find the test, the test will find you. Old people have tests. Young people have tests. Pastors and preachers and lay people have tests. Rich people and poor people have tests. Celebrities and common people have tests. You have been conditioned to taking tests ever since you were in grade school. Even in the first grade, you received the vocabulary words on Monday, then the week culminated with a spelling test on Friday. It is a fact of life. The test is normal.

Don't be surprised or even shocked when the test comes your way. Expect it. Prepare for it. The old saying goes, "When you're thirsty, it's too late to think about digging a well." Remember, it's not *if* the storm will come, but *when*. I recall, growing up in Michigan, when the leaves would begin to turn colors of autumn. When the weather would grow chilly, my father would take down the screen doors that stood in the front entry of our home during the summer. He would replace them with storm doors that did a great job of keeping Michigan outdoors. Winter was just around the corner, and her whipping winds were serious. It may be summer time in your life right now, but be advised; the bitter cold of winter is not far behind.

A few years ago a very significant test came to knock on my door. But on the other side of that test I learned that God can use those tests we think we have totally failed to launch our most significant successes. As I look back on that season of my life, I believe God had prepared me to climb this rocky mountain.

In July of 1984, after I left the teaching profession, I attended a music conference for Christian musicians that convened out in the beautiful Rocky Mountains of Colorado. The week was filled with workshops and competitions designed to educate and inspire those in the music ministry. I entered the competitions in the songwriting and vocalist categories. By week's end I went home with a third-place trophy in the vocal competition.

Several hundred other people had competed that week. To secure third place was quite an accomplishment. But as I left the conference, the enemy wasted no time in using my accomplishment against me. He whispered, "You're not only a third-place singer, you're a last-place singer. Last place is nothing but average. You're the best of the worst and the worst of the best. You'll never amount to anything."

These words preoccupied my thoughts all the way home and into the following weeks. By the middle of August, I was filled with regrets. I rehearsed in my mind what I could have done and what I should have sung. One day as I was walking through my home, I heard the voice of the Holy Spirit whisper a word of truth into my heart. "One day all of these earthly competitions will be over. Your accomplishments and trophies will not mean anything. The only thing that will be of any significance is worship at the feet of the Lord Jesus. Strive to win trophies of grace, the lives of people, who will enter heaven because of your influence."

Immediately I heard in my mind the strains of a melody and lines of a lyric that would change my life forever. With very little songwriting experience, I sat down at the piano that day to pen the song "All Rise," which has become, no doubt, the signature song of my entire music ministry and career. I began singing the song in my home church. The music minister recognized the potential in the song and had it arranged for our choir to sing in an upcoming Southern Baptist evangelism conference.

The evening finally came, and when it was time to sing, I stepped out from the alto section to sing the solo. The glorious strains of music from the choir and orchestra rang throughout the sanctuary, and the presence of the Lord filled the room in a powerful way. The congregation responded with a standing ovation that seemed endless. We sang "All Rise" again. This time, people stood up all over the auditorium. Many were in tears. Many began to lift their hands in worship. When the song concluded, the people continued to worship God with shouts of praise. I remember one young preacher who shouted and threw his Bible into the air. I'd never witnessed anything like this in a white Baptist meeting. By the end of the night we had sung the song four times. The service had been videotaped. The recording of the service began to circulate throughout the convention, and my telephone began to ring with requests to come to churches to sing "All Rise." A song born out of a last-place experience became the vehicle that God would use to open doors to churches all over the world. Out of what I considered a loss came the song that has basically propelled this ministry.

As you walk by faith and not by sight, you will trip and may even fall, but remember God is working behind the scenes to cause even your failures, your stumbling blocks, to become steppingstones that will elevate you to higher places. Your misery could very well launch your ministry.

THE TEST IS NECESSARY

Just as the testing process is a normal part of a life headed toward maturity, testing is essential for refining your life or exposing defects. In the life of the believer, God uses a time of testing to produce humility, to cleanse us and to teach us. It is important to remember: *The test is necessary.*

Trials reveal your quality and develop character. They disclose what you are made of. They will either bring out the best in you, or they will bring out the worst in you. Take an inventory of your own life right now. What are you made of, my friend? Are you well put together? Does your life exhibit strength like that of tightly woven fabric, which is resilient and enduring? Or do you buckle underneath the pressure every time a challenge comes along? Let's look at what the apostle Paul has to say about it.

> But we also glory in tribulations, knowing that tribulation produces perseverance; and perseverance, character; and character hope.
>
> —ROMANS 5:3–4, NKJV

Picture a scientist in a laboratory. The researcher goes through systematic methods of evaluation so that he might discover new knowledge. This usually means organized scientific testing. During the testing process, the scientist looks for impurities that must be isolated and removed. Aren't you glad that the laboratory puts your medicines through a battery of tests before they are put on the market and you purchase them by prescription or over the counter? Because of testing, we enjoy a higher standard of living.

> *God is working behind the scenes to cause even your failures, your stumbling blocks, to become steppingstones that will elevate you to higher places.*

Do you recall the story of the Wright brothers? They invented the first aircraft. But their discovery did not come without hardship. The Wright brothers' maiden voyage was preceded by numerous test flights. Some test flights were a total disaster. But each test was necessary, because it allowed them to eliminate the things that were not working and isolate those things that worked. And after many tests, many disastrous attempts, they finally produced a plane that would fly.

Let's look at it this way. If you have ever gone shopping for a new car, you drove onto the lot of the dealership to take a look around. You spotted a car that you liked. You admired the style, the color, the tires and the wheel covers. You even got inside and checked out the touch and the smell of the brand-new leather interior. You adjusted the seats to fit your posture. You examined the dashboard and all the other bells and whistles. But if you were a serious buyer with a down payment in your purse, you asked the car salesman if you could take the car for a *test drive*. During the test drive, you saw and felt how the car actually performed under real driving conditions. Any car can look pretty on the showroom floor. But what really counts is how it performs when the rubber meets the road.

When you are faced with difficult challenges and you don't have answers to your questions, as you trust in God the answers will come.

This is why we undergo testing, so when the pressure is on we will produce favorable results, results that are pleasing to God. I have found in my own life that a particular test I was facing drove me to a greater dependency on God, a deeper intimacy with God and greater love for God. Your tests are necessary to remove impurities, to prepare you to endure life's twists and turns. You'll navigate the hills and valleys of life's obstacle courses and fly above the storms in your life. So remember, anything of value is tested. When you are faced with difficult challenges and you don't have answers to your questions, as you trust in God the answers will come. *The test is necessary.*

THE TEST IS NOTHING TO FEAR

The average student can go to grade school, middle school, high school and college. But someday that student must get out there in the real world and apply what was learned all those years. We must be tested and proven so that when the storm comes—and they will—we will be able to stand. My mother has often said, "You are either in the storm, coming out of the storm or headed for another storm." If you are prepared, then you have no reason to be anxious. So, remember: *The test is nothing to fear.*

First John 4:4 says, "The one who is in you is greater than the one who is in the world."

God has equipped you with whatever you need to be an overcomer. You do not need to succumb to the enemy's schemes and devices. Sometimes life's trials take us by surprise. Even then you can be rooted and grounded, unmoved and unshaken. The apostle Peter offers us a tremendous word of encouragement:

> Dear friends, do not be surprised at the painful trial you are suffering, as though something strange were happening to you. But rejoice that you participate in the sufferings of Christ, so that you may be overjoyed when his glory is revealed.
>
> —1 PETER 4:12–13

In Georgia, when we have even the mildest storms, pine tree limbs litter the street. Georgia pine trees have many branches. When storm winds blow, falling branches do lots of damage to electrical wiring and rooftops.

But palm trees that line the coast of Georgia are a different breed of tree. When hurricanes blow through the coastal part of our state, houses are blown off their foundations. Hotels and beachfront property are washed away. Windows are shattered into bits and pieces, and cars are overturned. But have you noticed that even in the midst of strong winds that exceed more than one hundred miles per hour the palm tree is still standing? Even after the storm has passed the palm tree remains unscathed. What is the difference between the pine tree and the palm tree? The palm tree has a tap root system that goes deep into the ground and wraps itself around the foundation of the earth. Oftentimes, the trunk of the palm tree, which can sometimes be as wide as five feet in circumference, goes deep within the earth. This root system allows the tree to bend but not break, giving it great resistance and resilience in the fiercest storm. Psalm 1:3 says that if we meditate on His Word day and night, we shall be "like a tree planted by streams of water, which yields its fruit in its season and whose leaf does not wither. Whatever he does prospers."

Difficulties are certain to come. You may be navigating a personal storm at this very moment. But you have a choice as to how you will handle this situation. You can be like the pine tree, coming apart and losing control, injuring yourself and those around you. Or you can be the palm tree. Even with your back bent, you don't even think about breaking or coming apart in the face of the storm. You are anchored strong and secure. On the other side of the storm, you will still be standing.

Now, let's take a look at two different kinds of students you will find in the classroom of faith. Hopefully you are not the kind of student who likes to procrastinate. Do you know the procrastinator's motto? "Why put off for tomorrow what can be done the day after tomorrow?" This student knows the test is coming, but he continues to put off the inevitable. Before he knows it, it's the night before the big semester exam. He is forced to stay up all night and burn the midnight oil. The next day he is exhausted from lack of sleep and enters the classroom nervous and unprepared. During the test he doesn't quite remember the correct answers, so he just guesses. Needless to say, he leaves the classroom very discouraged because he knows he has not done his best. Ultimately, this student will receive a failing grade.

Let's look at the next student. Hopefully, this will sound familiar to you. This student has been a hard-working student all semester long. Consistent and methodical study habits have been practiced. He has shown up for class and completed all homework assignments. He has learned to apply his knowledge to practical situations. What was not understood, the teacher was asked to explain. He came to class early or stayed late to get extra help from the teacher if necessary. When exam day came, that student had the usual pre-test jitters, but he felt good and was ready. He was able to walk into the classroom, sit down in the assigned seat and take the test with confidence.

The ideal student is obvious. The consistent, methodical student who knew the test was coming and prepared for it in advance is the one who came through with a passing grade. This student will have no problem even when surprise pop quizzes are announced.

The same applies to students of the Word of God. This principle has been underscored throughout this book. The one who knows the Word of God and applies it to her life is the one who will pass the test. The ideal student commits God's Word to memory and acts upon it when tests come.

So do you want to know how to pass life's test with confidence? Begin by committing Psalm 119:11 to memory. "I have hidden your word in my heart that I might not sin against you."

Do you want to know how to keep your feet firmly planted on shaky ground? Start now by memorizing Proverbs 3:5–6: "Trust in the LORD with all your heart and lean not on your own understanding; in all your ways acknowledge him, and he will make your paths straight."

How do you guard your heart against anxiety in a world that

shudders with fear? What do you do when you encounter another one of life's emergencies and you need heaven's 911 in a hurry? Remember Philippians 4:6–7: "Be anxious for nothing, but in everything by prayer and supplication, with thanksgiving, let your requests be made known to God; and the peace of God, which surpasses all understanding, will guard your hearts and minds through Christ Jesus" (NKJV).

What do you do when you need the 411, the correct information concerning life's questions? Remember 2 Timothy 2:15: "Be diligent to present yourself approved to God, a worker who does not need to be ashamed, rightly dividing the word of truth" (NKJV).

God has made available to you everything that you need to pass any test you encounter.

What kind of student are you? I pray that you are the faithful one who relies on God to be your source of strength. Even death, the ultimate test, is nothing to fear because Jesus has taken the sting out of death. Someday, you don't know when, you will have to take the biggest exam of your life, and it will be your final exam. It's going to be the exam that you have studied for all your life. You can be filled with the certainty that you will see Jesus, either by death, or you will meet Him when He returns. But one day, if you have been faithful to Him, by receiving Jesus as your personal Savior, you will receive your reward. Second Corinthians 4:17 says, "For our light affliction, which is but for a moment, is working for us a far more exceeding and eternal weight of glory" (NKJV).

Remember, the difficult circumstance you are facing right now is a test. It's only a test. God has made available to you everything that you need to pass any test you encounter. Tests are normal. Everybody must take them. They are common to the Christian walk. You are not alone on this journey. Tests are necessary. They come to refine, renew, reprove and reform. As you encounter them, the result will be less of you and more of Christ. There is no testimony without a test. Your experience will ultimately help someone else along the way. Tests are nothing to fear. A good teacher will equip the student with everything she needs to know to pass even those tests that seem to take you off guard.

The next time you are faced with one of life's difficult tests, whether it is for a moment or for a season, remember that if you are prepared, you can walk into the classroom of faith, sit down to take the test without fear and pass with flying colors.

That is why, for Christ's sake, I delight in weaknesses, in insults, in hardships, in persecutions, in difficulties. For when I am weak, then I am strong.

—2 CORINTHIANS 12:10

CHAPTER 12

Faith

for the Fragile

N O MATTER HOW hard we try to avoid it, life will sneak up on your blind side like a 210-pound linebacker, catch you off guard, attack and hold you in its grip like a vice. Then it will throw you down on the playing field of life and leave you with the very wind knocked out of you.

As everyone knows, there is little we can do to escape tragedy. No amount of money can buy a guarantee that we'll flee from its grasp. It is always lurking around the next corner, and the enormity of it always takes us by surprise. One day the executive businessman is living large in his office with a penthouse view, a hefty salary and plenty of perks. The next day he gets the news that his company is bankrupt, and he has lost his job and his pension. The wife with three children and a house in the suburbs carts her children off to private school in the morning, only to receive a phone call that afternoon from her doctor that the mammogram has come back showing signs of cancer. The couple who move to the country to live minimally, to get away from the noise and pollution of the city, find their crops have failed for lack of rain. When it comes to trial and tragedy, the prince and the pauper are brothers. It doesn't matter who you are or what you do or don't do for a living.

Tragedy doesn't care who you are.

What do you do when life takes you by surprise? How do you put things back together when the world is falling apart all around you?

King David was no stranger to catastrophe. Even though he was king over all of Israel, with servants at his beck and call and riches at his disposal, tragedy struck David's house in monumental proportions. Much of David's misery was brought on as a result of his own bad decision making. Regardless of how David's life ended up in shambles, he illustrates that money, power and influence can often control people, but God always has the last word.

In 2 Samuel 11 we discover that David lusted after a beautiful woman named Bathsheba. She was the wife of Uriah, a general in David's army. David, wielding his power, summoned Bathsheba to his palace. An innocent visit turned into a guilty pleasure, and King David had an affair with Bathsheba while her husband, Uriah, was off fighting in the war at King David's command.

What's done in the dark will surely come to the light. Bathsheba became pregnant. Then David had Uriah killed so he wouldn't find out about David's misuse and abuse of power at his wife's expense. Soon after Uriah's death, David married Bathsheba. A few months later, a son was born to them. Talk about making your bed and having to lie in it. David's actions bore devastating and irreversible consequences. According to 2 Samuel 12:13–15, God's judgment was that the child would be stricken with an illness and would ultimately die.

During the child's illness, David begged God to save him. "David pleaded with God for the child. He fasted and went into his house and spent the nights lying on the ground. The elders of his household stood beside him to get him up from the ground, but he refused, and he would not eat any food with them" (2 Sam. 12:16–17).

I can picture David crying out to God for the life of his child. I can hear him coming to grips with his sinful actions and their devastating consequences. I can almost imagine how King David must have felt. His heart was certainly filled with remorse and regret. Can you see King David, a man known as a mighty man of valor, now reduced to weakness and vulnerability? I'm sure that he would have traded his entire kingdom to change his circumstances. Like any loving parent, David would have traded his own life for the life of his son. During those tremendously trying days as David lay on his face before God, what we now know as Psalm 51 was his heart's cry.

> Have mercy on me, O God,
>   according to your unfailing love;
> according to your great compassion
>   blot out my transgressions.
> Wash away all my iniquity
>   and cleanse me from my sin.
>
> For I know my transgressions,
>   and my sin is always before me.
> Against you, you only, have I sinned
>   and done what is evil in your sight...
>
> Create in me a pure heart, O God,
>   and renew a steadfast spirit in me.
> Do not cast me from your presence
>   or take your Holy Spirit from me.
> Restore to me the joy of your salvation
>   and grant me a willing spirit, to sustain me.
>
> —PSALM 51:1–4, 10–11

David's heart was truly crushed. The Bible says that David was sorry for his adulterous affair with Bathsheba and for having her husband put to death in an attempt to cover up his deeds. After seven days of fasting, the child died. David's servants reluctantly delivered the news of the child's death (2 Sam. 12:19). "Then David got up from the ground. After he had washed, put on lotions and changed his clothes, he went into the house of the LORD and worshiped. Then he went to his own house, and at his request they served him food, and he ate" (v. 20).

I once heard a speaker give a wise word of warning to people in the ministry or in leadership positions. He developed what he called *The H.A.L.T Theory.* He told the people that the enemy is looking for the weaknesses and places of vulnerability in your life. He advised the people never to get too…

HUNGRY
ANGRY
LONELY
TIRED

God's Spirit ministered that truth to David's heart. It was at this point in his life when King David made a life-changing decision. He did not continue to lie down and dwell in his own self-pity. No doubt, in his heart, he wanted to give up, but by faith, he moved himself into the act of living again. The Bible says *he got up.* In other words, he was willing to live above his situation. He would not become a victim of his circumstances—he became a victor over them. After his week of mourning, weeping and confessing, David knew that his sins were forgiven and that God had a plan for his future. He was determined to move on with his life.

After he got up, *he washed.* It was time to live in the present. That meant putting the past in its place. Where does the past belong? It belongs in the past. Put it there. Keep it there. Not only was David keenly aware that his past was forgiven, he knew he could start all over again with a fresh, clean slate. He rejoiced in the fact that with God, the pages of sin are all torn out and God is not somewhere keeping score. God is the Giver of the second chance, a third, a fourth, a fifth—or however many chances you need until, with His help, you get it right.

Next, *he put on lotions and changed his clothes.* David refreshed himself not only by changing his clothes, but also by changing his mind. It was imperative that David put on a new frame of mind. David realized that if he was to be an overcomer, he would have to get a new mind-set, a new attitude. God would give him everything he needed to start over again. David needed a brand-new start, and God granted it.

Then, David went to the house of God and *worshiped.* David left his house and went to God's house. By taking his eyes off his sin, he was able to focus on God's forgiveness. This is such an important point because this is where so many of us get stuck. We are convinced that because we cannot forgive ourselves, God cannot forgive us, either. We're convinced that we don't deserve His forgiveness. Well, I've got news for us all. *We don't deserve it.* Forgiveness is wrapped up tightly in a gift called *grace.* You can't buy it. You can't perform for it. You must open up your heart and receive it as a gift.

> *David needed a brand-new start, and God granted it.*

When you add it all up, David, like all of us, had plenty of reasons to loathe himself. But David knew firsthand the power of God's unfailing love and great compassion. When we are in God's presence, we realize how awesome and sinless and holy

God is. And in that same light, we see how wretched and sinful and unholy we are. The first step toward an attitude of true worship is realizing that there is a God, and we are not Him.

Then *he went to his own house.* David went back to his house to face the music that would begin to define the future. He had the choice to sing a dry, woeful, funeral dirge. Instead, David would begin to sing a new song, a melodious and hopeful ballad. It took a lot of courage to return to the scene of the crime, so to speak. But in doing so, he proved to himself and to everyone else that he would not allow shame to rule his life, his house, his heart or his future.

Finally, *at his request…he ate.* David realized that if he would enjoy the promise of hope for tomorrow, he would need strength for today. God had refreshed his mind and spirit. So David would have to take responsibility for nurturing his body. David went back to the business of living. He also went back to the basics of working and serving his God and the people of Israel. God was true to His Word—eventually David and Bathsheba had other sons. Their fourth son was named Solomon.

In God's time, Solomon became the next king over Israel. He left us a written legacy in the form of three of the Bible's greatest Books—Proverbs, Ecclesiastes and Song of Solomon. His practical words of wisdom would cause Solomon to be known as the wisest man who ever lived.

King David's son King Solomon said these words:

> As fish are caught in a cruel net,
>   or birds are taken in a snare,
> so men are trapped by evil times
>   that fall unexpectedly upon them.
>
> —ECCLESIASTES 9:12

Tragedy visits everyone's house. Lock the doors and the

windows if you want. It doesn't matter. Tragedy will find its way in. Disaster visited my friend's house. Her husband died suddenly of a heart attack. I called her on the phone the night before her husband's memorial service. I didn't really know what to say to comfort her after her husband's sudden death, but I knew we would find comfort in hearing one another's voices. As if by rote, I asked the question, "How ya doin'?"

She said some words that gave both of us strength. She said, "I'm doing fine, for the moment. But that's all I can ask for, is strength for the moment. I know I can depend on God to get me from one moment to the next, from one activity to the next, from one day to the next."

All that God requires of us is that we trust Him from one moment to the next.

"Problems are only opportunities in work clothes," Henry Kaiser said.[1] Maybe the crumbled mess at your feet comes as a result of your own bad decision making. Or maybe life just tip-toed up behind you and pulled the rug out from under you when you weren't looking, leaving you in the middle of a mess of grief and despair. Either way, God is able to bring redemption to your circumstances. If you will allow Him, God will pick up the pieces of what seem to be ruins and make something out of them.

TRIUMPH OUT OF TRAGEDY

This past year, I began telling a new story in my concerts. It's the story of a sweet, young, black couple who moved up north to Michigan from Mississippi in the mid-1940s. Escaping poverty, discrimination and prejudice, they settled in a small town where the husband found work. He was called to preach, and later to pastor a small church work there. Over the years, their family and church grew. Members were added to their church and to their family.

They had two sons when their third child, a daughter, was born. They were experiencing the blessings of God. But tragedy visited their house. Their newborn daughter was born with *hydrocephalus*, a disease known as *water on the brain*. Doctors didn't offer much hope and warned of the side effects of the disease and the impending surgery. They predicted that a shunt would have to be inserted to relieve pressure on the brain.

The prognosis was grim. Their daughter could be severely handicapped mentally and physically or could even receive the death sentence. This precious couple, with their backs against the wall, had nowhere to look but up. They trusted their daughter to God and the surgeons. On the day of the surgery, the doctors were amazed. The swelling had subsided, and the shunt that they predicted was necessary would not be needed. They relieved the pressure on her tiny brain.

After spending a few days in the hospital, this little baby girl went home to face an uncertain future. But triumph won over tragedy. That little girl grew to be a healthy toddler, then a star student, graduating from high school and college with honors. Today she is a wife, mother, grandmother, teacher, singer, songwriter, author, talk-show host and encourager. That little girl was me—Babbie Mason. God took what started out as a tragedy and turned it into a triumph.

Every once in a while as I am combing my hair, I will run my fingers over the long scar that travels from the top of my head, down the left side of my head to just above my left ear. As I trace the raised scar, I'm reminded of the faithfulness of God. What the devil meant for my demise, God turned around and worked it for my good and for His glory. There's no pain anymore, only a scar. Scars can be ugly and shameful, but not this one. This scar reminds me that even before I knew I was in the world, God smiled on me and made me a recipient of His favor. This scar reminds me that it doesn't hurt any more. This scar reminds me that I'm no longer sick and close to death, but I am alive and healed. I'm saved, and I'm on a mission.

What tragedy have you suffered in the past that you're still trying to get over? What crime did you commit that came back to haunt you? What loss have you endured that has left your heart and your house a little emptier? Do you wear an ugly scar, physically or emotionally, from past trauma? Take courage, my friend. You are the person God wishes to use to display His strength. Don't keep your head low to the ground. Hold your head up high, and rejoice in the fact that when you are weak, that is when Christ in you is strong.

All that God requires of us is that we trust Him from one moment to the next.

Elisabeth Elliot said it best: "When things happen which dismay, we ought to look to God for His meaning, and remember that He is not taken by surprise, nor can His purpose be thwarted in the end."[2]

Two are better than one,
  because they have a good return for their
  work:
If one falls down,
  his friend can help him up.
But pity the man who falls
  and has no one to help him up!
Also, if two lie down together, they will
  keep warm.
  But how can one keep warm alone?
Though one may be overpowered,
  two can defend themselves.
A cord of three strands is not quickly
  broken.

—ECCLESIASTES 4:9–12

CHAPTER 13

Fan the
Faith

THE WEEK THAT our oldest son was to be married was a week filled with mixed emotions. All the sweet memories of his childhood came flooding back to me in waves that were bittersweet. We planned to fly to Colorado where his bride-to-be lived with her family. He would fly out midweek, and the rest of the family would meet him there that weekend. The night before he was to leave, I wanted to have one last conversation with him. Deep in my heart, I felt that dads not only gave their daughters away on their wedding day, but moms gave away the precious gift of their sons, as well.

He was marrying a precious young lady, the kind of woman that a mother prays would marry her son. I was excited about his future and about seeing him go out on his own to start a family. But just for one more moment I wanted to hang on as tightly as possible. I wanted to tell him how proud I was of him. I wanted him to know that it had been a blessing for us as parents to raise him and watch him grow up. I wanted to assure him that we would be praying for him and for his new family every day.

The moment I opened my mouth to deliver my "I love you and I'm proud of you" speech, not a word came out. My throat closed off, my eyes welled up and all I was able to do for the next few minutes was hold my son in my arms and cry. At that moment, words would have gotten in the way. Tears said it all.

That weekend, the wedding was beautiful. I sat there on the front row next to my husband, Charles. I was as cool as a cucumber. A river of tears had flowed all that week, and I think I was all cried out. Our son was so handsome, and his bride was just beautiful. Sitting there, I was able to smile at them, enjoying the moment. I glanced over to catch the eye of my husband to find *him* crying like a baby!

We look back on that moment, and we laugh—now. We look back on a lot of moments and laugh. Like the time when I ran out on the football field after our youngest son got hurt during a play. Another time, while we were on the road the same son had gotten away from us after the concert. While we were talking, hugging necks and signing autographs, he and a friend slipped outside to play. When we finally found them, they had shimmied up a lattice trellis and were playing on the roof of the city's civic center. Another memory reminds me of the first summer that Charles and I were married. We were, as Charles would say, "so poor we couldn't pay attention." One day, Charles cooked a hearty but inexpensive meal. He cooked what I call a "beige meal." We ate beige meat, with beige gravy, white rice and white bread. The only colorful thing on the table was a glass of red Kool-Aid for each of us.

Our personality differences have created lots of memories and have left lots of room for laughter. The city girl that I am, my country-boy husband has tried to show me the importance of canning and freezing so I can fill the pantry full of his homegrown vegetables. He envisions me picking blackberries and making preserves and fruit pies. I am willing to give it a try, but I insist on wearing gloves so I don't risk getting blackberry stains on my acrylic nails. Out at our farm, he takes me on his rounds to feed the fish, the chickens and the pigs. I don't think I will ever completely trade in my city upbringing, but it will be fun giving it a try.

Early in our marriage, I began noticing that my husband had an unusual speech mannerism. Without his knowing, he mispronounces words from time to time. He thinks he's saying a certain word correctly, and while he comes close, he ends up so far away. He thinks he's saying one thing when, in actuality, he is saying something quite different. Funny, I never heard this speech pattern before we were married, which proves that love is not only blind, but it is also deaf and mute.

As a former English teacher, songwriter and lover of words, I felt it was my duty to help Charles hone in on his communication skills. He didn't appreciate my help, but that didn't stop me from trying. Once we passed a church early one Saturday morning. The parking lot was filled with cars. We were in a quandary as to what might have been going on at a church so early on a Saturday morning. As we passed the church's marquee, Charles remarked, "Oh, it's a Seventh-Day Advantage Church. Saturday is their Savage day, ain't it?" I knew he meant to say *Seventh-Day Adventist Church* and *Saturday was their Sabbath Day.*

One day, Charles was retelling a story of a huge fire in downtown Atlanta. New loft apartments had caught on fire and were quickly going up in flames. He said, "Man, the heat from the blade was so intenth that some firemen were overcome by smoke insulation." I know he meant to say, "The heat from the *blaze* was so *intense* that some firemen were overcome by smoke *inhalation.*" There used to be a day when I would get very frustrated in my efforts to correct his phonetics. Today God has graced the situation, and now I can sit back, relax and listen to my husband tell a good story. Sometimes, I even chuckle when he mispronounces a word that strikes me funny.

Around our house, we've even given his mispronounced words a name. We call them *Masonisms*. Charles is sure to put a smile on all of our faces whether he realizes it or not. Once, I asked him how a football player became a candidate for the Football Hall of Fame. He said, "Well, you have to be old and abducted."

Be certain that whenever you have opposites, with a positive and a negative charge, sparks will fly.

We have established quite a history together. The good times have been really good. But there have been some difficult times, too. Charles would be the first to agree with me that marriage is hard work. Coming to an agreement at all has been the challenge for us. We can joke about it now. But, basically, during most of our marriage we have agreed to disagree. It has been both amazing and frustrating at the same time. If I saw something as black, Charles would see it as white. If Charles saw something as an opportunity, I saw it as a risk. If I wanted to vacation in the city, he wanted to go to the country.

In the beginning of our marriage, our differences became the thorn in the side of our relationship. We are quite opposite in our personalities. That is what attracted us to each other, but that also is what frustrated us. I have often said in response to that, "Not only do opposites attract. They attack, as well. Be certain that whenever you have opposites, with a positive and a negative charge, sparks will fly." Our disagreements were not intentional. We just saw things from different points of view.

If you are married, then that may be true of your marriage, too. One of you stays up late. The other goes to bed early. One is a neat nut. The other is drawn to clutter. Concerning sex, one is a keg of dynamite; the other is a dud. One says, "Let's." The other says, "Let's not." One likes chocolate. The other likes vanilla. If you are different going into the marriage, you can expect those differences to intensify once you cross the threshold, for sure.

Early in our marriage, we looked at our differences as liabilities. We wondered if we would ever see eye to eye on anything. We were a lot like Jane and Steve.

> There was a handsome young man named Steve who married a beautiful young woman named Jane. Steve was fun loving, adventurous and impulsive. He loved living on the edge and thinking off the cuff. A free spirit, it didn't bother him if the house was a bit messy. There would always be time to clean the house and get organized. Let's live for the moment.
>
> Jane, on the other hand, was conscientious and ambitious. She had graduated from college with honors and took pride in her accomplishments. She took her job as a CPA seriously. Above all, she liked order. In the beginning of their relationship, Jane was drawn to Steve's cavalier attitude about life and his ability to be spontaneous. After they married, when she wanted him to make order in their home a priority, she felt that he failed her miserably. When he came home, he dropped his tie on the nearest chair, draped his shirt across the bedpost and kicked off his shoes at the foot of their bed. Then he would suggest that they go to play a game of tennis.
>
> When Jane complained, Steve would put his clothes and shoes in the right place. She made sure he was

aware of her displeasure, but within a few days, he would revert to his old messy patterns. Before long, Jane became so resentful of his lack of appreciation for order that she resented his invitation to play tennis. She began to lecture him, saying, "How can you think of going out to play tennis when you haven't done your part of the work around here?"

Steve began to accuse her of treating him like a child. Before long, Steve no longer made any effort to keep order, and playing tennis together became a thing of the past. Their differences had become their worst enemy.

LET GOD FIX YOU

Charles and I don't play tennis, but I recognized some of our behavior patterns in Jane and Steve's relationship. Charles and I work in the ministry together. Our relationship was often strained at home because of something that happened at the office. Or we'd find decision making almost impossible at the office because of difficulties at home. Either way, living together was challenging. We tried fixing each other. Pointing out each other's mistakes was a frequent occurrence. That only made matters worse. Although there was no doubt that we loved each other, we didn't seem to like each other very much.

Marriage expert Dr. Gary Chapman says that when this happens, it is important for couples to remember that love is not a feeling. "Love is the attitude of thinking that says, 'I choose to look out for your interests. How may I help you?' Love is a way of thinking and behaving…It's not necessary to have warm feelings in order to express love."[1]

Dr. James Dobson, author and founder of Focus on the Family, says that there are several outside forces that are certain to hinder the marriage relationship:

☕ Overcommitment and physical exhaustion will lead to agitation and discouragement. Couples should avoid becoming too busy or too overloaded with work to spend needed time together.

☕ Money mismanagement will put a strain on the household finances and the marriage, too. Be careful not to overextend your finances or max out your credit cards.

☕ Unrealistic expectations are a trap to any marriage. We come into the marriage anticipating rose-covered cottages, walks down primrose lanes and uninterrupted joy. Expectations produce conflict.

I wish we had that information going into our marriage. After the honeymoon period was over and reality set in, we found it difficult to communicate. Our disagreements turned to discord. That did nothing but introduce contention and strife into our home. No one wants to be in a marriage where there is always discord and disagreement. But that's exactly where we were. Instead of responding to each other's needs, we reacted to defend our own individual arguments. Our marriage became strained.

To be honest, for a while, staying married was really hard. It's interesting. When the heat was really on, pressure brought out the worst in us. But we were determined to make it work. We decided that we would never bail out of our marriage. Too many times we have seen couples bail out of the marriage while going through the stormiest season of their marriage. They just throw up their hands and throw in the towel.

Picture that in the natural sense. If you and your family were out fishing and a storm rose up, you wouldn't jump overboard and tell everybody to jump overboard with you, would you?

No! You'd do everything within your power to save your vessel and the lives of everybody on board. If the vessel was in danger of sinking, you'd go to work quickly to keep water out of the boat. You'd use a radio to call or signal for help. You'd make sure everyone had a lifejacket. You'd make absolutely certain that your spouse and the children were safe. You'd never consider just giving up and jumping in, leaving everyone to survive the best way they could. Jumping out of the boat in the middle of the storm is an invitation to disaster for everyone involved.

I heard a lady jokingly say of her marriage of over fifty years, "I have never considered divorce. Murder, yes, but never divorce." She knew then what I know now. Divorce is not an option. But if I could be quite honest with you, it's not like the thought didn't cross our minds. We just couldn't go through with it. We were raising a beautiful family, and our ministry was a blessing to countless numbers of people.

As long as there are people in marriage, there will always be a potential for struggle.

Satan would have loved to see us throw all that away. We knew in our hearts that we wanted to keep our marriage and our family intact. We knew that if our marriage ended in divorce, our family would be destroyed, our ministry would be damaged and many people could get hurt. We were afraid of the message it would send to people like you who read my books and listen to my music. Were we going to trust God to help us, or were we going to throw it all away?

We determined in our hearts that divorce would never be an option. We were aware of the statistics. And we did not want to be one of them. We knew that Christians lead the way to divorce court. And we decided we would be Christians who trusted God instead. We also knew that 80 to 90 percent of people who remain married were happier and healthier than people who get divorced. We would not give up. I learned a long time ago that hurt people hurt people. As long as there are people in marriage, there will always be a potential for struggle. We would trust God to empower us to clean up what we messed up.

When you're tired of fighting and you come to a place of surrender, that is the place where God will meet you to fix things. We went to work on ourselves, not each other. We stopped pointing fingers at each other and started examining our own heart. We received some excellent Christian counseling. This experience opened our eyes and gave us tremendous insights into our personalities and how our personal makeup influences our relationship.

The Holy Spirit ministered to me that I should work on me and leave Charles in the hands of the Lord. Immediately, I became aware of some areas I needed to work on. Getting my point across has never been a problem for me. Unfortunately, that works against me sometimes. The Holy Spirit convicted me that working on my words would be a good place to start. So I began to pray, asking God to help me guard my tongue and to speak words to build Charles up instead of tearing him down.

My problem was that I had gotten in the habit of using discouraging words instead of encouraging ones. I heard it said once, "Often the difference between a successful marriage and a mediocre one consists of leaving about three or four things a day unsaid." With the help of the Holy Spirit, I would endeavor to speak less and listen more. Criticize less and compliment more. Complain less and celebrate more. Instead of always trying to prove my point, God would help me to yield to my husband's thoughts and ideas.

When Charles married me, I knew he was marrying Mrs. Right. But I didn't have to be Mrs. Always Right. In other words, I often thought my ideas were best. What I learned is this: I don't always have to have the last word. I needed to stop interrupting my husband before he completed his sentences. Proverbs 18:13 says, "He who answers before listening—that is his folly and his shame." Ouch! The Bible is tight, but it's right!

Proverbs 15:1 says, "A gentle answer turns away wrath, but a harsh word stirs up anger." It wasn't long before I found the promises from God's Word beginning to work on me and in me. I saw they were working on my husband, too. This is a sweet season in our marriage. We are allowing our differences to work for us and not against us.

All of this is painful to admit. I wish I could say our story went something like this:

> Boy meets girl. Boy dates girl. Boy spends money that he doesn't have on girl to buy girl a huge diamond ring. Boy proposes. Girl accepts. Boy marries girl. Boy buys girl a split-level house. Boy and girl have 2.5 kids and a minivan with wood paneling on the side. Boy and girl live happily ever after.

The Cleavers and the Huxtables exist only on television. In real life, real stuff happens. I'm not telling you this to let you in on the not-so-pretty stuff in my life. I'm sharing all of this with you because I believe that if you are married, God can use our experience to strengthen your marriage. If you're single, then let our experience serve as signs along the roadside. If it doesn't help you in any way, then share our story with someone you know who can benefit from it.

CELEBRATE THE VALUE OF YOUR SPOUSE

I don't know exactly when it began to happen, but gradually, little by little, we began to feel the winds of change blow through our home. As time went by, we realized that each person had something of value to contribute. Many times I found that the ideas Charles brought to our collaborative projects were better than mine. We were on our way to appreciating each other. We would soon learn that appreciation leads to celebration.

> *God has taught us to forgive*
> *Time has helped us to forget*
> *Faith will show us how to live*
> *Without regret.*

Today, not only is our marriage stronger, but we are friends. We enjoy being together. We've learned that what we once thought of as a weakness has really turned out to be the best feature our marriage relationship has. Because we see things from different perspectives, we are more likely to cover every base. I value deeply Charles's contributions to our marriage and to the ministry that God has entrusted to us. Yes, we have both made some terrible mistakes along the way. But God has taught us to work them out through loving and forgiving.

I recorded an album in 2001 that was titled *Timeless*. As a songwriter, God had begun to inspire some songs of a different style than I had written for record projects in the past. Still with Christian lyrics, the Lord began to give me songs that had a 1940s classic Jazz and Big Band flavor. At first, I wondered if this was really a God idea. When the Lord inspired me to write a love song to my husband, a song celebrating Christian marriage, I knew that was the deciding factor. It became a prayer that God would take that song and use it to encourage people to stay married regardless of their marital circumstances. Here are some of the words:

> After all this time together
> Looking back across the years
> Through sunshine and stormy weather
> We're still here.
>
> When we crossed over troubled waters
> It was God who brought us through
> And after all this time
> I still believe in me and you.
>
> God has taught us to forgive
> Time has helped us to forget
> Faith will show us how to live
> Without regret.
>
> We'll let nothing come between us
> And I'll spend my life to prove
> That after all this time
> I still believe in me and you.[2]

That song has become a tangible way for me to express my love for my husband. Other couples have told me it's done the same for them.

Earlier this year Charles needed a written biography on him.

The Chamber of Commerce in our city bestowed upon Charles the high honor of Volunteer of the Year, and they needed some information concerning his community involvement. So I wrote his biography. As I listed his accomplishments, I became more and more impressed with him. I was reminded of characteristics and values in him that I appreciated. I thought to myself, *I'd really like to get to know this person better.* I'd like to give you that same assignment. Sit down and write a positive biographical sketch of your spouse. Maybe you'll see a side that you haven't seen before.

God wants to transform your marriage relationship from a rocky fortress to a beautiful jewel that will reflect His love and compassion.

If your marriage is facing hard times or your relationship is just a little stale, let me offer a suggestion. Here are five ways to give your marriage a needed faith lift:

1. *Wake up.* Each day is a brand-new opportunity to invest in your marriage. Don't bring up old and hurtful issues. Avoid holding grudges. "This is the day the LORD has made; let us rejoice and be glad in it" (Ps. 118:24).

2. *Stand up.* Fight for your marriage. Always defend your spouse. Never belittle him, but find ways to elevate his spirit. Always remain loyal to your husband. Commit to being partners for life. Build your partner up with your words instead of tearing him down. "Better to live on a corner of the roof than share a house with a quarrelsome wife" (Prov. 21:9).

3. *Hold up.* Even when you don't feel like you're in love—act like it. It is easier to act yourself into a way of thinking than to think yourself into a way of acting. You will endure the dry spells if you remember love is not something you feel—it is something you do. "Love is patient, love is kind. It does not envy, it does not boast, it is not proud. It is not rude, it is not self-seeking, it is not easily angered, it keeps no record of wrongs" (Cor. 13:4–5).

4. *Lift up.* Nothing heals the hurts in a marriage like prayer. Praying for and with each other douses out the flames of contention. God will honor the humility that prayer produces in a heart. It's hard to pray and remain angry. When disagreements arise, lift up a prayer. "Therefore confess your sins to each other and pray for each other so that you may be healed. The prayer of a righteous man is powerful and effective" (James 5:16).

5. *Look up.* Marriage is God's idea. Always keep Him at the very center of your home. The closer each of you is to God, the closer you will grow to each other. A marriage of intimacy and passion is directly related to one's personal relationship with Jesus. Keep the fires burning in your vertical relationship, and your horizontal one will be natu-

rally affected. "Whom have I in heaven but you? And earth has nothing I desire besides you. My flesh and my heart may fail, but God is the strength of my heart and my portion forever" (Ps. 73:25–26

Have you ever wondered how, over time, something that felt so right in the beginning could begin to feel so wrong? Did your marriage start out in an ideal way, but it ended up being a major disappointment? As you look back on things, did you start out in the center lane, cruising right along, but something along the way caused your marriage to sidetrack? Has the thought of divorce ever crossed your mind?

Take it from us. We know how you feel. But there is hope and grace for your marriage. Don't wait for your spouse to change. Allow God to start with you. If you are like a wrecking crew with your words, begin to build your loved one up with kind words instead of tearing him down. Don't factor God out of your marriage. Ecclesiastes 4:12 says, "A cord of three strands is not quickly broken."

My pastor once said that if you want to remove wrinkles from fabric, you have to apply heat and pressure. Be sure of this: Opposition will come against your marriage. But when you and your husband are tightly wrapped around the love of God, outward pressures and heated situations can bring out the best if you ride the storm with Jesus and don't bail out. You do have a choice. You can treat your marriage as precious, or you can throw it all away. Remember that your marriage is a treasure. Together, you start out as a diamond in the rough. Diamonds are found deep in the earth embedded in rock formations. A diamond must be excavated from dirt, sand and gravel. Then it is crushed, sorted, cut and polished. Over a period of time, with lots of pressure, God wants to transform your marriage relationship from a rocky fortress to a beautiful jewel that will reflect His love and compassion. Trust God to turn your marriage into something beautiful.

Ponder this thought: A great marriage is one where you fall in love over and over and over again, always with the same person.

A good tree cannot bear bad fruit, and a bad tree cannot bear good fruit. Every tree that does not bear good fruit is cut down and thrown into the fire. Thus, by their fruit you will recognize them.

—MATTHEW 7:18–20

CHAPTER 14

Faith

Your Fruit

A YOUNG BLACK MAN and his wife had been farmers for years and had a commendable work ethic. They lived in the rural Louisiana town of Fort Necessity. After the turn of the twentieth century, black people in the South continued to feel the oppressive brunt of prejudice and discrimination, even though slavery had been abolished. More often than not, they were taken advantage of and treated with cruelty and disrespect.

But this young couple fought hard to rise above racism and segregation with persistence and hard work. These young people were sharecroppers. A sharecropper is a tenant farmer, found mostly in the southern region of the United States, who is provided credit for seed, tools, living quarters and food. Sharecroppers work the land to receive an agreed-upon share of the value of the crops, minus any charges that may accrue during the year. The agreement, however, was not usually slanted in favor of the tenant. The black tenant and the white landlord would "settle up" at the end of harvest time, which was usually at the end of the year and close to the holiday season. Invariably, the charges always exceeded the credit, keeping the poor tenant in a constant state of debt to the white landlord. This young couple faced this reality on a daily basis.

This farmer and his wife had a houseful of children. They raised fourteen children on a tenant farmer's income. Large families were quite common during this time. Some of the children, generally the older ones, had to miss many days of school because they were needed as field hands. They helped to get the crops planted, plowed and protected by harvesting them before the fall rains came. In spite of these difficult circumstances, thirteen of the fourteen children managed to graduate from high school. Beyond this accomplishment, this family was dedicated to God and their church and rarely missed a Sunday worship service.

This hard-working couple believed in demonstrating the messages of hard work and faithfulness to their children. Furthermore, the father not only believed in providing for his family, but he also enjoyed providing for the community. Each year, he would plant a garden that he referred to as the Family Garden. He would tell the community that they could have all they were willing to harvest. The community welcomed this kind man's generosity. This husband-and-wife team believed the secret to their garden's success came as a result of three things. Without fail, each time the Family Garden was planted, they *planted* and then they *prayed*. Then they watched God *produce*. The Family Garden is still producing today, and I'm told that you would have to see the harvest to believe it. For years, the entire community has enjoyed the tomatoes, cucumbers, collard and mustard greens, pears and plums in bounteous supply. This hard-working family knew firsthand that God's work done in God's way will never lack God's supply.

LESSONS FOR LIVING GOD'S WAY

This couple's diligent lifestyle exhibits some lessons we would all do well to learn. As farmers do, they rose well before the sun came up and worked long and hard day after day in the hot summer sun. This couple was *disciplined*. These hard workers had no tractors or modern farming equipment to turn over the hard and crusty soil. They worked the fields by the sweat of their brows and the callousness of their bare hands. They were *diligent*. I'm sure they had to pray often for favorable weather conditions. No doubt they had to use plenty of creative ingenuity and common sense to keep pests and animals from eating their crops. They were *practical*. Then in due season they would harvest their crops with the hope that there would be enough to feed their family through the winter months and pay off their debts. They were *prayerful*.

God sees you as a fertile field that is ready to receive good seed, get continuous nurturing from God's Word and ultimately produce good fruit for His kingdom. God has a purpose and plan for you. He has given you a measure of a gift that should represent Christ here on earth. People are watching your life. When people see you, do they see Christ in you? God's Word tells us, "Each one should use whatever gift he has received to serve others, faithfully administering God's grace in its various forms" (1 Pet. 4:10).

Some people feel that their gift should be used solely for their own personal fulfillment or gain. Others feel that they don't possess any special gift at all. When you use your gifts to serve others, people are blessed in return. They will, in turn, thank God for the help that they have received from you. When you use your gift to serve others, you are blessed as well. People receive help, you are encouraged, and God gets the glory.

What does it mean to be fruitful? God told Adam and Eve to be fruitful (Gen. 1:28). Initially, you might think that being fruitful relates only to procreation. But this does not apply only to having children. If that were the case, then those who are single, male or past childbearing years would be left empty-handed. But this passage can also be interpreted to mean spiritual fruit. The command to be fruitful applies to every believer.

God sees you as a fertile field that is ready to receive good seed, get continuous nurturing from God's Word and ultimately produce good fruit for His kingdom.

God has given each of us an assignment. I know for certain that if God gives you an assignment, then He will provide all you need to fulfill that work. I have often heard it said that where God guides, He provides. I found out that fruit bearing always follows faith planting. When Jesus gave the charge to the disciples in Mark 16 to go into all the world and preach the gospel, they obeyed. Look down a little further in Mark 16, and you will read: "…the Lord working with them, and confirming the word with signs following" (Mark 16:20, KJV). When you and I act in faith in all of our efforts to please God and to produce fruit, God is committed, according to His promises, to fulfill His Word.

Being fruitful means living a life that gets results. Every believer should desire to live a life that is effective and pleasing to God. The fruit farmer, at first glance, may be concerned about the appearance of the leaves on his fruit trees. He can tell by looking at the leaves if the tree is getting enough sunlight, food and moisture. But like this farmer, God is not ultimately looking for a tree with beautiful leaves. He is focused on fruit. You may mistake talent for fruit. You may mistake fame for fruit. You may think that if a person has a nice car, dresses well or has "the look," he or she is fruitful. But fruit does not develop from the outside in. It is the quality of character and service to others. God is looking for people whose lives will generate godly fruit. He wants to entrust us to produce the fruit of the Spirit, which is love, joy, peace, patience, kindness, goodness, faithfulness, gentleness and self-control (Gal. 5:22–23).

Whenever God plants, He does it with a finished objective in mind. From the very beginning, God wanted to have fellowship with man. He knew man would fail and that He would have to send Jesus to us to bring about reconciliation. God has always had a plan for man. The very word *planting* begins with the word *plan*. All effective and eternal planting must first be planned. God plans for you to accomplish something specific and extraordinary with your life. He has given you a certain ability that, when combined with the Holy Spirit's help, will allow you to be fruitful and productive. God never intended for you to live a life of mediocrity. He does not want you to live beneath your privileges, to merely exist. He longs for you to experience life and life to the fullest. The world may define abundant life in terms of money, sex and the accumulation of things. But God desires that we live a life of real meaning and purpose.

Matthew 7:16 says that we will recognize people by their fruit. The King James Version says, "Ye shall *know* them by their fruits" (emphasis added). It doesn't say, "You shall know them by the way they dress, by their credentials, by their social status

or talents." You will know people *by the results they get through
the lives they live.* Matthew 7 talks about false prophets who
spoke only what the king and the people around them wanted
to hear, yet claimed their messages were from God. False
prophets are just as popular today. Jesus warns us to be on the
alert for those who speak words that sound religious but, in all
actuality, are empty and ineffective words. Popularity, money
and fame motivate these words. The messages from people like
these are all about the people—not about Christ. Remember
that a bad tree cannot produce good fruit.

*God plans for you to
accomplish something
specific and extraordinary
with your life.*

A good farmer cultivates only those trees that are producing
fruit. Those that do not produce fruit are replaced. Don't you
love it when you see nature's laws line up with spiritual principles? This is exactly what God's Word says to those who do not
remain in Him.

> I am the vine; you are the branches. If a man remains
> in me and I in him, he will bear much fruit; apart from
> me you can do nothing. If anyone does not remain in
> me, he is like a branch that is thrown away and withers;
> such branches are picked up, thrown into the fire and
> burned.
>
> —JOHN 15:5

Fruit comes as a result of maturity. I once heard someone say that you can't plant a seed one night and pick the fruit the next morning. Developing good fruit takes time. Don't get frustrated when you don't see fruit for your labor when you think you should. This may not be your season. Be patient. Continue to water the seed of God's Word that has been planted in your life, and continue to wait on God. I know that being in God's waiting room is hard. But you have to remember that God is working behind the scenes and under the surface. In God's time, you will reap a harvest.

How are your gardening skills developing right now? What is growing in your spiritual garden at this moment? Do you have a beautiful garden that is flourishing? Do you, like that sharecropping couple, have a garden that is so beautiful that you just want all the neighbors to enjoy it? Or perhaps your spiritual garden is struggling. Perhaps your garden has been overtaken with weeds and debris, and you don't know what to do.

PREPARE YOUR SOIL

I learned a great lesson in gardening one spring. Let me share with you what I learned. On the side of our house we have a small spot where, from time to time, Charles would grow a few tomatoes. Each year he would set out a few small plants, and each year he'd get a good crop of ripe, red tomatoes. However, one spring after setting out a few plants, nothing seemed to grow in that spot other than weeds. The weeds easily overtook the small plants. During this time, one of our neighbors came over, saw my husband's predicament and offered to help. This neighbor had a lot of experience with gardening because he had been a landscape contractor for many years. He saw the potential in that spot and believed that it would produce fruit. So he went right to work on that spot!

The first thing he did was *faith the roots*. My neighbor had to *see* tomatoes before he *saw* tomatoes. He had to envision that fruit would grow in that little garden spot long before anything was planted. But that plot of land had some challenges. My gardener friend had to break up some fallow ground. Do you remember the parable of the sower? (See Mark 4:1–8.) Some of the good seed fell by the wayside, on stony ground, among thorns. The ground on the side of my house was stony!

As my neighbor began to dig, he found rocks and even pieces of cement from the adjoining sidewalk that had crumbled and worked their way beneath the ground! It was no longer a mystery why only weeds would grow there. So he took a shovel and turned the soil over. At the same time, he removed all the large rocks and pieces of cement. Then he took the garden tiller and tilled the soil thoroughly. He added fertilizer to the soil in his final preparation stage before planting. After he had weeded and fertilized, he left the rest to my husband, Charles, who put small tomato plants in the soil. This time the tender roots began to anchor themselves by wrapping their tendrils around the soil while pushing their way up toward the light. This time the roots of these plants were able to penetrate the ground.

My neighbor had to see tomatoes before he saw tomatoes.

Paul prayed a passionate prayer for the church at Ephesus "…that Christ may dwell in your hearts through faith. And I pray that you, being rooted and established [grounded] in love …" (Eph. 3:17). Just as the stones had to be removed from my garden spot in order for it to produce fruit, so will the stones have to be removed from your heart in order for you to produce spiritual fruit.

I encourage you, my friend, to roll up your sleeves, get out your tools and ask God to break up the hard, stony places in your heart. The Master Gardener will rid the soil of your heart from bitter roots that have wrapped themselves around anger, resentment and painful memories. As the Holy Spirit, who is your helper, rids your life of the things that are choking out your peace and your joy and the other fruit of the Spirit, you will begin to flourish like a mighty oak tree. I know you will grow and exceed your own expectations of fruitfulness.

Keeping a garden free of weeds and debris is difficult. But I learned to pray a "Ten-Finger Prayer," found in Philippians 4:13 (NKJV). I extend both hands upward to God and pray as I count:

1. "I
2. can
3. do
4. all
5. things
6. through
7. Christ
8. who
9. strengthens
10. me."

As the tomato plants began to flourish, sprouts and shoots began bursting forth everywhere. I just knew that the more sprouts and shoots that appeared, the more tomatoes we would have. Well, that was not the case. Charles began to cut off and pluck out many of those sprouts and shoots. I grew concerned. He said he was plucking the "suckers" off the main stalk so that the plant will produce larger tomatoes. It was in that moment I saw a sermon! We had to *faith the shoots*.

Remember the parable of the vine and the branches? John 15:2 states, "…while every branch that does bear fruit he prunes so that it will be even more fruitful." Pruning is not a pretty process. As a matter of fact, pruning is a painful process. Those vines and stems were pretty to me with all their shoots, but they had to be pruned in order for them to be productive. What is the main purpose for pruning? Pruning focuses the plant and brings it into greater fruitfulness.

I had to learn that sometimes plants must be *trained* so they can develop uniformity and strength. Training may involve propping up the stems or tying up the tree's branches. Or the training period may consist solely of pruning, which will strengthen the plant by cutting away any of its unproductive parts. Psalm 1:3 says that we are like trees. There may be times in your life when God wants to train you for greater service. Or there may be some things, even some people, that you may have to cut off because the relationship may be toxic.

Faith is our day-to-day, minute-by-minute and moment-by-moment response to what God promises and to what God has already done!

Don't resist God's correction and instruction. Instead, give in to Him. Draw near to Him. Delight yourself in His wisdom, and meditate on it day and night. You will find yourself "like a tree planted by streams of water, which yields its fruit in season and whose leaf does not wither. Whatever he does prospers" (Ps. 1:3). The word *meditate* means to mutter or to murmur. I encourage you, as you go about your day, to rehearse or practice speaking the Word of God to yourself. Whisper it softly to yourself as you walk through your house or go back and forth to your car. As you memorize the precepts of the Word of God, those principles will sink deep down into the fertile soil of your heart. You will find that as you enter into a crisis situation, even a time of personal pruning, the Word that is in you is what will come out of you.

Faith is our response to God's promises! Faith is our day-to-day, minute-by-minute and moment-by-moment response to what God promises and to what God has already done! If we could lock into this principle, we would see greater fruitfulness in our lives. A seed is a beautiful demonstration of faith. When the planter places the seed in the ground, the seed simply responds to the environment and produces. As believers, that's all we have to do in order to be fruitful. Remember, never pull up in unbelief what God has planted in faith.

At the right time, in the right season and when all conditions are right, the tree will bear *fruit.* Your life and ministry take the same course. If you want to be fruitful and multiply your gifts, you must allow the seed of God's Word to fall upon the fertile soil of your heart. In other words, you have to *faith your fruit.* Don't miss any opportunities to nurture and build up your faith walk with prayer and devotion. You will find your life being rooted and grounded and not easily moved by changing circumstances. You will endure the processes of propping and pruning. As you are faithful with little, God will entrust you with much. You will begin to see results that will change you and impact the lives of those around you.

The moment those tomatoes were planted in that garden, faith began. From the moment those plants went into the ground, we anticipated seeing tomatoes. We made plans for the tomatoes. We found new recipes for the tomatoes. We planned to give some away. We believed those plants would produce fruit. Sure enough, as time went on, fruit came forth.

What seeds have you planted in faith recently? What dreams and visions are you nurturing and anticipate holding in your hand someday? Maybe your spiritual garden is struggling. Perhaps your garden has been overtaken with weeds, and you don't know what to do. Examine the soil of your heart today. Are there rocks, stones and bricks of bitterness? Are you struggling with a load of stones that is causing you to stumble in your walk? Perhaps you are carrying in your purse a few rocks of resentment. Be it a brick, stone or rock, they all will cause the soil of your heart to become hard and unfruitful. They will hinder your faith, and no spiritual fruit will be able to grow in your garden.

The more you operate in your purpose, the stronger you become.

Simply pause and be still or quiet before God. Ask Him to show you the soil of your soul. Ask Him to do this only if you are willing to confront what He shows you. After He has shown you, then cry out for His mercy and grace, and ask Him to take away everything within you that is not like Him. Ask Him to take away anything that would hinder you from growing spiritually and getting to know Him.

Have you ever heard of anyone planting apple seeds and harvesting plum trees? This just will not happen. God has designed it so that every seed has within itself the blueprint for its identity. When that seed sprouts and becomes a plant, within the plant lies the plan for its own fulfillment. Basically we reap what we sow!

Take another look at the tree in Psalm 1. Think of all the things that trees do. Trees provide shade for those who are overheated from the tensions of life. Trees provide a place to rest for the traveler who has grown weary on the journey. Trees provide a place to play and, for a moment, forget the cares of life. Trees provide fuel to warm hearts that have been wounded and grown cold and indifferent. Trees provide shelter for those who have been in the storms of life and need a covering. And trees provide fruit for those who are hungry and long to be fed. People will be impressed with the leaves on your tree, but when they get up close, they will begin to look for fruit. When the love of God nurtures a tree, it will be fruitful and the fruit will remain.

God will make you fruitful if you ask Him. Ask God to show you your gifts. God has given each person the gifts he or she can use to fulfill God's purpose. Generally, other people will confirm to you what you already know within to be true about yourself. When I first starting singing I knew within my heart that I loved music and wanted to serve God in this capacity. Along the way, other people recognized the gift within me and encouraged me.

Ask God to give you opportunities to use your gift. It is very important to trust God to open doors for you. Don't get ahead of God and push doors open prematurely. Colossians 4:3 says, "And pray for us, too, that God may open a door for our message." When asking God for direction, we should look for those areas that ignite a passion within us. For some that might be helping the poor. For others it might be helping single parents or reaching the lost. Whatever excites you is a good indicator of your direction.

Along with finding that direction will come confidence. When you are doing what you are supposed to be doing, you have courage and confidence to work through the obstacles. The more you operate in your purpose, the stronger you become.

Anyone can count the seeds in an apple. Only God can count the apples in a seed. God believes in adding and multiplying. Allow Him to use your life for His glory and for your joy. Don't be concerned about developing pretty leaves. Press on toward maturity. Don't get anxious when things don't seem to go your way. Continue to be faithful. Show up for work with the gift you have in your hand. Be encouraged by these words from God's Word:

> So let's not allow ourselves to get fatigued doing good. At the right time we will harvest a good crop if we don't give up, or quit.
>
> —GALATIANS 6:9, THE MESSAGE

Therefore, since we are surrounded by such a great cloud of witnesses, let us throw off everything that hinders and the sin that so easily entangles, and let us run with perseverance the race marked out for us. Let us fix our eyes on Jesus, the author and perfecter of our faith.

—HEBREWS 12:1–2

CHAPTER 15

Faith

Your Finish

I T'S NOT HOW you start the race, but how you finish." There is a great deal of truth to that statement. Olympian Derek Redmond immortalized those very words in the 1992 Olympic Games in Barcelona, Spain. One of Britain's greatest 400-meter runners, Derek Redmond had trained long and hard for the Olympic semifinals. Plagued by injuries, he had endured eleven operations on his Achilles tendons throughout his running career. Despite setbacks, he was determined to make a mark in Olympic history.

On the day of the race, Derek Redmond lined up with seven other runners at the start-up line. He was mentally focused. He had his eye on the finish line. He was the favorite among sports enthusiasts to take home the gold. All eyes were on him. One hundred thousand people watched from the stands, millions by television. The gun fired. Derek had one of the best starts ever in his running career. As he approached the halfway mark, Derek heard something snap in his right leg. A setback he had experienced before, he knew immediately he would not finish this race. The other seven runners passed by him with lightning speed. It was like a bad dream. He had been in this same place before, after suffering injury to his Achilles tendon in the

1988 Summer Olympic Games in Seoul, South Korea.

Seconds later, the race was over almost as quickly as it had started. The winners were decided, but Redmond was not among them. He had collapsed on the track, 250 meters from the finish line. He was sprawled across the lane and writhing with pain. He managed to pull himself up from the track and, in spite of immense pain, began to stagger painstakingly toward the finish line.

Remember, it's not how you start, but how you finish.

Watching from the stands was Derek's biggest fan—his father, Jim Redmond. He watched his son as he struggled. Jim Redmond could take it no longer. He left his seat in the stands and hurried down to the track. Past the medics and past security, this father was just as determined to reach his son as his son was to reach the finish line. As his son hobbled down the track, Jim Redmond finally caught up with his son. As they met, the injured sprinter crumpled into the arms of his father. As the father helped the son collect himself, he embraced his son and became his support to help him finish the race. The two crossed the finish line together.

What a way to finish! Derek Redmond truly demonstrates what a true champion looks like. It's amazing that he made his mark. But not by winning the race. He made his mark in history by losing the race but winning the battle. That race will go down as one of the greatest moments in Olympic history. It was one of the most viewed pieces of film ever watched by American audiences. Few remember who won the gold medal in the 400-meter race that day. But the picture of a strong father and a son at his weakest is emblazoned in our memories. Remember, it's not how you start, but how you finish.

WATCH YOUR COACH

We are not all Olympians, but all of us have a race to run. We are all in this race called *life*. If you are anything like me, you wonder some days how you can continue to put one foot in front of the other. The race is challenging. Sometimes in life, there are steep hills to climb. Sometimes on really high mountaintops the air is thin and the climate is so dry you can hardly breathe.

But there is One who goes before us to show us how to run. Jesus Christ has already run this race and won the prize. He is the Author, the Creator of our faith, and He is the Finisher of our faith, or the completion of our faith. The King James Version puts it this way: "Looking unto Jesus the author and finisher of our faith." I love how the Message Bible puts it, too. "Keep your eyes on Jesus, who both began and finished this race we're in." The Modern Language Bible says, "With our eyes on Jesus, the cause and completer of our faith."

Jesus is there in the beginning to teach you, to coach you. As He coaches you, He runs the race with you to remind and reassure you that you are not alone. And He stands at the finish line to celebrate and reward you. According to John 1, He was with God in the beginning, and He will always be there. Wherever you are, right now, He is there with you. So, as you run, read His Word and pay attention to His running style.

When you get weary from the race, don't carry the burdens that you've picked up along the way. Cast them over on Jesus. He really cares for you (1 Pet. 5:7). Get rid of sin, the baggage in your life. I heard someone say recently that we must "get light." That is just what we must do. Read again Hebrews 12:1:

"…let us lay aside every weight, and the sin which doth so easily beset us, and let us run with patience the race that is set before us" (KJV).

In 1996 the Summer Olympic Games were held here in our city, Atlanta, Georgia. I have never seen so much excitement in our city in all the years my family has lived here. The streets were decorated with banners. Flowers and beautiful trees were planted. A gorgeous park was constructed. People from all over the world came to our hospitable city, the Queen of the South. During that time, Atlantans as a whole caught Olympic fever. Everywhere you looked, people were decked out in Olympic garb. Sweat shirts, T-shirts, warm-up suits and caps became the desired wardrobe.

I do not consider myself an athlete by any means. But even I sported my Olympic attire. During the games, I sat in my living room on my nice cushy sofa in my warm-up suit and ate popcorn and drank a soft drink. I even imagined that I could be like them. Now, as excited as I was about the games, there was one big factor that separated me from the athletes. I was on the sofa. They were in the game!

At this stage, I think it's safe to say that I will never be an Olympic runner. But I do have life's race to run, and you do, too. I want to be successful at it. I will run so I can receive the prize. And I hope you do, as well.

If you want to receive a great reward, first you have to *get in the right race*. Philippians 3:14 says, "I press on toward the goal to win the prize for which God has called me heavenward in Christ Jesus." Your reward is in heaven with Jesus. Your reward is not here in this world. Your adversary the devil would like you to think that stuff—houses, land, cars and money—is your reward. But Matthew 6:19 says:

> Do not store up for yourselves treasures on earth,

where moth and rust destroy, and where thieves break
in and steal. But store up for yourselves treasures in
heaven, where moth and rust do not destroy, and
where thieves do not break in and steal. For where
your treasure is, there your heart will be also.

I saw a bumper sticker once that said, "He who dies with the
most toys wins." Let me clear something up. He who dies with
the most toys only leaves them behind for someone else to play
with. Don't forget—your reward is in heaven.

*To get into life's meaningful
and purposeful race, the first
thing you have to do is start.*

The race that will end in heaven is the only race worth running. It is the greatest race any runner could ever run. It's bigger than the Olympics. The race starts with Jesus and ends with
Jesus. If Jesus is not your goal, if He is not your reason for running, then you're in the wrong race. As a matter of fact, if
you're not running for Jesus, then it's not a race at all. It's a rat
race. It's a maze. Like a laboratory mouse, you run around in
circles, with no purpose or goal in sight. You may be running
fast. But you'll be in a hurry to get nowhere. If you don't know
where you're headed, how will you know how to get there?

To get into life's meaningful and purposeful race, the first
thing you have to do is start. That may be the hardest part. If
you have received Jesus Christ as your Lord and Savior, then
you are on the right track. If you have never said *yes* to Jesus'
invitation, then now is the best time to accept His invitation.

Don't wait another minute. Perhaps Nike said it best: "Just do it." Make Jesus your Lord. In Joshua 24:15, the Bible says, "Choose for yourselves this day whom you will serve."

If you want to get in the race here's what you must do. Ask Jesus to come into your heart right now by praying to Him. If you have trouble finding the words, pray this prayer:

> *Dear God in heaven, come into my heart. Forgive me of my sin. I acknowledge and accept Jesus Christ into my life. I give Him full control to be my Master and Lord. Thank You, Lord, for saving me. Amen.*

The moment you prayed this prayer, God heard you and granted your request. "The Lord is not slow in keeping his promise…not wanting anyone to perish, but everyone to come to repentance" (2 Pet. 3:9). God has a plan and a purpose for your life. I want to encourage you to receive your calling, find your place and know your purpose. A good local pastor will be a tremendous help in this area. Now that you are on the Lord's side, you are in the race!

The next thing you must do in order to be a great and successful runner is *set your pace*. Too often runners are distracted by what other runners are doing in the race. Distractions will cause you to lose focus. Ultimately, distractions could cause you to lose the race, or you could become seriously injured. Setting your pace will give you the ability to concentrate and conserve energy until you need it most. If you run too fast, you will not last the entire race. If you run too slowly, you will risk coming in last. You must keep your eyes on the prize, not on the people around you. Watching how others run their race may cause you to lose yours. Don't compare yourself to others. In 2 Corinthians 10:12, the Bible says, "When they measure themselves by themselves and compare themselves with themselves, they are not wise."

Successful runners have the ability to focus like an eagle. They have exceptional vision and keenness. They are secure in their identity. They know who they are. They know that eagles don't fly with chickens and turkeys. Eagles don't roost—they soar! In their own unique, God-given style, eagles fly like nothing else. Great runners, like eagles, have an unwavering ability to endure for the long term. They stay in their lane and keep their pace.

In the race that you're running, have you been distracted by the cares of life? Have you questioned God concerning the course you are running? Maybe you are saying, "If only my circumstances were different. Then I could run faster and jump higher, and life would be different." This is the time for you to seek the Lord and ask Him to define your purpose. Everyone is a ten at something.

You have to work hard to achieve your goals. Remember who you are and whose you are. In your walk with God, you will have ups and downs, ins and outs, hits and misses. You will struggle with wavering and inconsistency. But the struggle will make you stronger. Running uphill will increase your stamina. So don't let the steep hills of life get you down. Look up for a faith lift. Psalm 121:1–2 says:

> I will lift up my eyes to the hills—
> where does my help come from?
> My help comes from the LORD,
> the Maker of heaven and earth.

HEAD FOR THE PRIZE

Stay on course by staying in God's Word. Stay in your lane by knowing who you are in Christ. Keep your eyes on Jesus. He is your prize.

Athletes live a life of discipline. They eat right. They get plenty of sleep. They let nothing interfere with their perform-ance. In other words, *they guard their space.* They are careful to discern who and what they allow to get close to them. That which you allow into your space ultimately becomes you. How many times have we heard it said, "If you lie down with dogs, you get up with fleas"? You may have heard another old saying: "Tell me who your friends are, and I will tell you who you are." The Bible says it another way: "Evil communications corrupt good manners" (1 Cor. 15:33, KJV). The Living Bible expresses it like this: "If you listen to them you will start acting like them."

The successful runner is very discriminating as to what comes into his ears, eyes and mouth. So you must be disci-plined. What you hear shapes your thoughts, what you see shapes your vision, and what you eat shapes your shape. In 1936, track and field star Jesse Owens made America proud by winning four gold medals at the Berlin Olympics where he set new world records in the 200-meter sprint and the long jump. This is what he had to say about his ability to guard his space and remain disciplined: "Every morning, just like in Alabama, I got up with the sun, ate my breakfast even before my mother and sisters and brothers, and went to school, winter, spring, and fall alike to run and jump and bend my body this way and that for Mr. Charles Riley."[1]

Mr. Riley was Jesse Owens' high school athletics coach. With determination and hard work, Jesse Owens, a black man from a poverty-stricken farm in Alabama, rose to become the first American, black or white, to win four gold medals in a single Olympics. He overcame segregation, racism and bigotry to prove to Hitler's Nazi Germany, and Americans as well, that African Americans have a significant place in the world of sports.

Do you feel that people around you are overstepping their

boundaries? Are there people in your space who are toxic and not contributing to your purpose? Maybe you have been hearing, eating and looking at the wrong things. Only you can turn that around by making choices that conform to the Word of God. Choose to become disciplined. Find someone to whom you can be accountable. Rebuild those boundaries by drawing the line at what you will and will not listen to. Set new boundaries on what you will and will not eat spiritually, maybe even physically. Set only clean things before your eyes. Philippians 4:8–9 says:

> Fix your thoughts on what is true and good and right. Think about things that are pure and lovely, and dwell on the fine, good things in others. Think about all you can praise God for and be glad about. Keep putting into practice all you learned…
>
> —TLB

Always remember that you were saved by grace. Now you must live and run this Christian race by grace.

Great and successful runners *run with grace*. It could be that your life has been a lot like Derek Redmond's. You train and practice. You practice and train. In some races you do well. In others you fail, sometimes miserably. In your Christian race have you ever had a moment when you felt like giving up? Have you been struggling with a habit that you can't seem to conquer? Maybe you have had times when you felt so close to accomplishing some spiritual goal, and suddenly disappointment reared its ugly head.

When you fall, keep in mind the truth that God's grace allows you, like Derek Redmond, to get back up again.

You are not the reason you are running. It's not about you. Don't be afraid to show others your scars. That will help others to see the real Star of the race, who is Christ. Just do it! Keep on running! Always remember that you were saved by grace. Now you must live and run this Christian race by grace. "For it is by grace you have been saved" (Eph. 2:8). Follow this advice:

> I would have you learn this great fact: that a life of doing right is the wisest life there is. If you live that kind of life, you'll not limp or stumble as you run.
>
> —PROVERBS 4:11–12, TLB

The ability to *see His face* and receive a crown of righteousness is the final attribute of a successful runner. Great runners will do whatever they have to do to win the prize. Just as a skilled runner runs for his country and displays his country's colors proudly on his body to identify himself, so we run for the kingdom of God. We wear the garments of praise as our identity to show that we belong to Christ. The kingdom of God is our homeland. In the Book of Isaiah, we see an example of Jesus fixing His eyes on the goal: "I set my face like flint, and I know I will not be put to shame" (Isa. 50:7). *Like flint* means set hard, like a rock, determined to be stable, solid and sound.

If you were to grade the quality of the Christian race you're running right now, how would you do? On a scale of 1 to 10, with 10 being the best, where would you stand? Do you still have the joy of your salvation? Are you going to church but doing spiritual activities for the wrong reasons? Maybe you would say that you have a form of godliness but no real meaningful relationship with Jesus right now. I would venture to say that you are not alone.

God awaits your return to Him. I suggest that you do as Jesus did, set your face on Him. I'm reminded of a great hymn of our faith:

> Turn your eyes upon Jesus,
> Look full in His wonderful face,
> And the things of earth will grow strangely dim
> In the light of His glory and grace.[2]

Jesus is the glory and the crown. He is the finisher. As a singer in the Christian music industry, I must be careful not to lose my focus. I must always be mindful of why and for whom I am singing. If I am not careful, I could forget why I am in the race in the first place. If I watch what someone else is doing and compare myself to them, I risk being disqualified. The world's way to look at it is to make the Dove Award or the Grammy Award the prize. I have been privileged to win two Dove Awards with fourteen Dove nominations. But if the awards become my goal instead of Christ, then they become idols. No disrespect to these great organizations, but as a believer, that is not my aim. You and I must remember why we are running.

The apostle Paul had a biography that would put us all to shame. He was a Hebrew of the Hebrews, a purebred. He was circumcised on the eighth day according to Jewish law. He was on a mission to persecute Christians and knew the law inside and out. But Paul laid his credentials down to gain Christ. In Philippians 3:8 he states, "I consider them rubbish, that I may gain Christ."

Olympian Jesse Owens said something I think we all could learn from. He was talking about how short the sprint really is:

> To a sprinter, the hundred-yard dash is over in three

seconds, not nine or ten. The first "second" is when you come out of the blocks. The next is when you look up and take your first few strides to attain gain position. By that time the race is actually about half over. The final "second"—the longest slice of time in the world for an athlete—is that last half of the race, when you really bear down and see what you're made of. It seems to take an eternity, yet is all over before you can know what's happening.[3]

Life is too short to run in vain. Run to receive the prize.

Isn't that just like life? It's here, and before you know it, it's over. "For what is your life? It is even a vapor that appears for a little time and then vanishes away" (James 4:14, NKJV). Life is too short to run in vain. Run to receive the prize.

Have you ever noticed that when Olympic athletes win, their coaches are right there on the sidelines to spur them on? That is exactly what Jesus is doing for us right now. He, along with a great cloud of witnesses, is cheering us on to finish our race, and to finish well.

As the apostle Paul was nearing the end of his life, he knew that he had been faithful right to the very end. Like Paul, we must prepare to live, but make plans to die. One day, if you have run well, meaning that you have lived your life for Christ, you will have the joy of meeting Christ face to face. You don't have to be a hero in the Hall of Faith like Paul or Abraham. (See Hebrews 11.) This great reward is for us all. If you are faithful in your running, you will be able to say, like Paul, "I have fought the good fight, I have finished the race, I have kept the faith" (2 Tim. 4:7).

All the hardships you have to endure and all the difficulties you have to encounter will be worth it all when you see Jesus. He will say:

> Well done, good and faithful servant! You have been faithful with a few things; I will put you in charge of many things. Come and share your master's happiness!
>
> —MATTHEW 25:21

It's not how you start the race, but how you finish. Run to finish well, my friend. Run to finish well.

Chapter 1: *Faith* FIRST

1. "Miners Stuck Together," CBSNews.com (July 29, 2002): retrieved from Internet November 15, 2002 at www.cbsnews.com/stories/2002/07/29/national. "Trapped miners braved harrowing conditions," CNN.com (July 29, 2002): retrieved from Internet November 15, 2002 at http://cnn.usnews.

Chapter 2: PASSING THE *Faith* ALONG

1 "Show Me How to Love" by Babbie Mason. Copyright © 1988 Word Music, Inc. (a div. of Word Music Group, Inc.). All rights reserved. International copyright secured. Used by permission.

2. Catherine Booth, "Expect to Receive the Holy Spirit." Retrieved from Internet December 5, 2002 at www.cybershelter.net/org/Booth/booth5.htm.

Chapter 3: THE FELLOWSHIP OF *Faith*

1. "A Mighty Fortress Is Our God" by Martin Luther. Public domain.

Chapter 4: *Faith* WORKS

1. Edward W. Desmond, "A Pencil in the Hand of God," an interview with Mother Teresa, *Time* magazine (December 4, 1989).

Chapter 5: *Faith* YOUR FOUNDATION

1. "CQDaily Archives: April 2000," retrieved from Internet November 22, 2002 at www.timothyreport.homestead.com/April2000~ns4.html.

2. "How Firm a Foundation," John Rippon's *Selection of Hymns*, 1787. Public domain.

Chapter 7: *Faith* YOUR FAILURES

1. "Love Is the More Excellent Way" by Babbie Mason and Turner Lawton. Copyright © 1996 by Word Music, Inc. (a div. of Word Music Group, Inc.), May Sun Music (admin. by Word Music Group, Inc.) and Turner Lawton Music (admin. by Integrated Copyright Group, Inc.). All rights reserved. International copyright secured. Used by permission.

2. "Amazing Grace" by John Newton. Public domain.

Chapter 9: *Faith* YOUR FRETTING

1. "Famous Quotes," The Ultimate Mickey Rivers Website: retrieved from Internet December 5, 2002 at www.mickeyrivers.net/famousquotes.html.

2. "Quotes (and other information worth remembering)": retrieved from Internet December 5, 2002 at www.prism.gatech.edu/~tem233v/quotes.htm.

3. "Horace, Horace Quotations, Horace Sayings—Famous Quotes," retrieved from Internet December 6, 2002 at www.home.att.net/~quotesabout/horace.html.

4. Kenn's mother wrote this song and sang it to him as a child.

Chapter 10: *Faith* YOUR FAMILY

1. Edith Deen, *Great Women of the Bible* (Uhrichsville, OH: Barbour and Company, 1959).

2. "O for a Thousand Tongues to Sing" by Charles Wesley. Public domain.

3. "Heritage of Faith" by Babbie Mason. Copyright © 1996 May Sun Music (admin. by Word Music Group, Inc.) and Word Music Inc., (a div. of Word Music Group, Inc.). All rights reserved. International copyright secured. Used by permission.

Chapter 12: *Faith* FOR THE FRAGILE

1. "Famous Quotes," Brainy Quote: retrieved from Internet December 6, 2002 at www.brainyquote.com/quotes/quotes/h/q101259.html.

2. "CQDaily Archives: September 1999," retrieved from Internet December 6, 2002 at www.timothyreport.homestead.com/september99~ns4.html.

Chapter 13: FAN THE *Faith*

1. Jim Mueller and Duane Careb, "Q&A: A Conversation With Gary Chapman, Part One" (August 2002): retrieved from Internet December 6, 2002 at www.growthtrac.com/artman/publish/article_63.shtml.

2. "After All This Time" by Babbie Mason. Copyright © 2001 Praise and Worship Works. ASCAP. (Admin. by Gaither Copyright Mgmt.) All rights reserved. International copyright secured. Used by permission.

Chapter 15: *Faith* YOUR FINISH

1. "Quotes by Jesse Owens," The Official Jesse Owens Web Site: retrieved from Internet December 6, 2002 at www.jesseowens.com/quote2.html.

2. "Turn Your Eyes Upon Jesus" by Helen H. Lemmel. Public domain.

3. "Quotes by Jesse Owens," The Official Jesse Owens Web Site: retrieved from Internet December 6, 2002 at www.jesseowens.com/quote2.html.

At BABBIE MASON MINISTRIES, we endeavor to be an encouragement through concerts, record projects, songwriting, books and public speaking, teaching, the television talk show, *Babbie's House,* and our annual Babbie Mason Music Seminar, an annual conference for singers, songwriters and worship leaders.

For more information concerning Babbie Mason Ministries, please contact:

Babbie Mason Ministries
971 Old Columbus Road
Bowdon, Georgia 30108
770-952-1443

You can also visit us online at
www.babbie.com